ETHIOPIA
&
HAILE SELASSIE

INTERIM
HISTORY

ETHIOPIA

&

HAILE SELASSIE

Edited by Peter Schwab

Assistant Professor of Political Science
State University of New York, College at Purchase

FACTS ON FILE, INC.   NEW YORK

ETHIOPIA & HAILE SELASSIE

Library of Congress Catalog Card No. 70-154631

ISBN 0-87196-193-8

9 8 7 6 5 4 3 2 1

PRINTED IN THE UNITED STATES OF AMERICA

CONTENTS

Page

INTRODUCTION

Ethiopia is an african kingdom ancient enough to have been mentioned in the Old Testament and described in the 5th century BC by the Greek historian Herodotus. The emperor of Ethiopia, Haile Selassie I, is a Christian ruler whose right to the throne is based in large part on his claim of descent from an African queen and a Jewish king whose diplomatic romance is alluded to in the bible. Haile Selassie rules as the very powerful—if constitutional—monarch of a country in which strong forces favoring modernization are locked in struggle with potent advocates of traditions going back to the earliest days of recorded history.

Despite the fame of Haile Selassie and the long history of his land, relatively few scholars have published works on Ethiopia. Compared with other countries in Africa, Ethiopia has been neglected. Still, a student of Ethiopia can find a few excellent books on the subject. Among them would be: Margery Perham's *The Government of Ethiopia; Haile-Selassie's Government,* by Christopher Clapham; Richard Greenfield's *Ethiopia: A New Political History; Wax and Gold,* by Donald Levine, and *Ethiopia: The Modernization of Autocracy,* by Robert L. Hess. In addition, there are several standard histories of the country. The purpose of this book is to fill some of the gaps left by the earlier works. Material for this book came from various sources. The editor has visited Ethiopia to study its institutions and people, and he thanks Adelphi University and the U.S. Office of Education for grants that made this travel possible. He has relied on his doctoral dissertation, *An Analysis of Decision-Making in the Political System of Ethiopia* (the New School for Social Research), in several sections of the book. And, as is usual in INTERIM HISTORY books, he has borrowed heavily from the record compiled by FACTS ON FILE.

1

The Monarchy

The Old Testament tells of an Ethiopian monarch, the Queen of Sheba, who paid a visit to King Solomon in Jerusalem. Tradition has it that this queen, known to the Ethiopians as Queen Makeda (Queen Bilqis in the Arab legend), gave birth to a son of King Solomon. The Queen of Sheba was said to have ruled from 980 to 950 BC, and then her son became King Menelik I of Ethiopia. In Ethiopia's Constitution of 1955, Article 2 institutionalizes this tradition:

"The imperial dignity shall remain perpetually attached to the line of Haile Selassie I, descendant of King Sahle Selassie, whose line descends without interruption from the dynasty of Menelik I, son of the Queen of Ethiopia, the Queen of Sheba, and King Solomon of Jerusalem."

The modern Ethiopian monarchy begins with Emperor Theodore II (Tewdoros, originally Lij Kassa), who ruled 1818-68. Theodore attempted to modernize the empire and began the struggle to place the monarchy on a permanent basis. He introduced modern firearms to Ethiopia; he attempted to abolish slavery, and he relied heavily on Europeans who held technological skills. His attempt to centralize the government by appointing governors loyal to him failed.

Menelik II (1889-1913) introduced modern communications to Ethiopia and instituted the system of ministerial advisers. A major act of his was the granting of a concession to the French government for the construction of a railroad line from French Djibouti to Addis Ababa. When Menelik II died in 1913 he was succeeded by his grandson Lij Yasu (Lidj Yassu), whose association with Islam alienated him from the Christian majority in Ethiopia. With support from Christian leaders, Ras (Prince) Tafari Makonnen of Shoa (who later adopted the throne name Haile Selassie) brought about Lij Yasu's downfall in 1916. Menelik's daughter Zauditu (Judith) was crowned empress, and Tafari became regent and heir to the throne.

Lij Tafari Makonnen was born July 23, 1892 in Harar province. His father, Ras Makonnen, was a first cousin and a close adviser to Menelik II. Tafari was educated by French Jesuits. As a youth, he so impressed Menelik II that, at 14, he was given the official court title *dejazmatch* ("commander of the door"). He succeeded to his father's post of governor of

Harar in 1910. In 1911 he married Wayzaro Menen, Menelik II's great-granddaughter. (Wayzaro Menen died Feb. 13, 1962.) They had 6 children.

From 1916, when he became regent, until 1928, Tafari extended his power, putting down several rebellions and building up a military force loyal to him. He established schools throughout the country and began a program of sending young Ethiopians abroad for study. In 1923 he won Ethiopia's admission to the League of Nations, and in 1924 he emancipated his country's slaves. In 1924 he also took his first trip abroad, visiting various countries in Europe. What he saw during his travels added to his belief that Ethiopia should be modernized. Subsequently, many foreign advisers were brought to the country to assist in economic and technical matters.

Tafari assumed the title of *negus* (king) Oct. 7, 1928. Empress Zauditu died Apr. 3, 1930, and Tafari was crowned emperor Nov. 2, 1930, taking the name Haile Selassie (Power of the Trinity).

Haile Selassie was described by Richard Greenfield in *Ethiopia: A New Political History,* as "small, with delicate hands and striking eyes. His skin was very light even for an Ethiopian, and his appearance almost Middle Eastern.*"

Since his accession to the throne in 1930 Haile Selassie has deeply influenced the political and economic development of Ethiopia. From an isolated entity Ethiopia, through the energies of the emperor, has become prominent in international affairs. The development of 2 constitutions, the semi-institutionalization of parliament, the centralized—decentralization of the central government, have been policies initiated and influenced by the emperor. Tax programs, once non-existent in the country, are now functioning (though disputed) programs in at least part of Ethiopia. An education system has been structured and expanded, and social programs have been instituted. Yet, as Gwendolen Carter stated in her foreword to Robert Hess' *Ethiopia: The Modernization of Autocracy:* "in the face of what needs to be done to reform agricultural practices, rural communications and health, the pace of change is agonizingly slow."

---

* "Some Ethiopians are quite as dark-skinned as any Africans, yet others are very pale indeed...." (Greenfield's footnote)

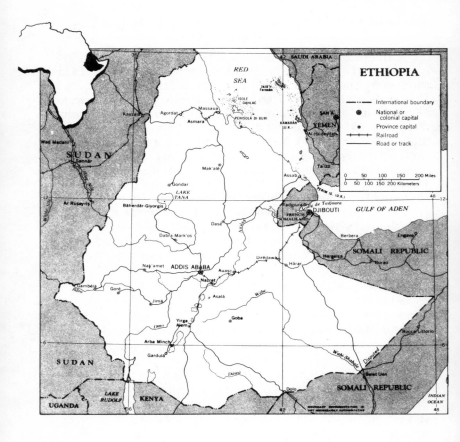

The Land & the People

Ethiopia occupies some 457,000 square miles of land in northeast Africa. It is bounded on the north by the Red Sea, on the east by the French Territory of the Afars & Issas (formerly French Somaliland) and the Somali Democratic Republic, on the south by Kenya and on the west and northwest by Sudan. Geographically diverse, the Ethiopian terrain is dominated by a high (6,000 to 10,000 feet) central plateau. Its Semien mountains in the north reach to a height of 13,500 feet. Ethiopia is also a land of many rivers, arid desert and coastal area. Ethiopia is the home of Lake Tana and its Blue Nile Falls, the source of the Blue Nile River. The Rift Valley cuts through the central plateau. The central plateau enjoys a temperate climate. Its principal cities, Addis Ababa, the capital, and Asmara, both located at altitudes of about 8,000 feet, have climates ranging from no lower than about 47 degrees F. to no higher than about 80 degrees F.

The country is divided into these 14 administrative units, or provinces: Shoa (location of the capital, Addis Ababa), Harar, Bale, Sidamo, Gamu-Gofa, Kaffa, Illubabor, Wollega, Gojam, Beghemder, Wello, Arussi, Tigre, Eritrea.

In the terminology of the 1970s, Ethiopia is an economically underdeveloped, or developing, country. Ethiopia has a per-capita income of approximately US$64 a year, and about 90% of the population earns a living from farming or livestock. The country's gross national product was about US$1½ billion (E$4¾ billion) in 1968. Ethiopia's major money crop, coffee, accounts for nearly 60% of the nation's exports, and Ethiopia is Africa's 4th largest producer of coffee. Skins, hides and meat are also exported, as are oil seed, oil cakes, fruit and vegetables, spices, the stimulant *chat* and civet (for perfume). Because of Ethiopia's machinery imports, the country runs a continual trade deficit. In 1968 exports were valued at US$105 million and imports at US$176 million. Ethiopia's major trading partners are the U.S., West Germany, Britain, Italy and Japan.

The population of Ethiopia is estimated at between 22 and 27 million. Throughout much of its history, the country has been ruled by the Amhara and Tigrai tribes, an elite minority who together constitute approximately ⅓ of the population and live in the northern provinces. Amharic, the major—and official—language of Ethiopia, is spoken by the Amhara, who, with the Tigrai, dominate the social, economic and political system. Both the Amharas and the Tigrais are Ethiopian Orthodox (Coptic) Christians. The largest ethnic group in Ethiopia, the Gallas, comprise some 40% of the population, speak Galla and inhabit the southern regions of Ethiopia (although some Gallas are also found in the north). The Galla people who reside close to the Muslims in the east have adopted Islam as their religion, while those living in the southwest have joined the Coptic Church. Some 40 other tribes and peoples, speaking various Semitic and Cushitic languages, also live in Ethiopia.

The Ethiopian Orthodox Church, in existence since the 4th century, is the established church of the empire. Its membership, made up almost entirely of the Amhara-Tigrai people, comprises 40% of the population. There is approximately the same percentage of Muslims in Ethiopia. The remaining Ethiopians are largely animists, although there is also a Judaic group, the Falasha. The Ethiopian Orthodox Church is one of the most powerful institutions representing tradition in Ethiopia. Resistant to change, the Church is one of the major countervailing political powers that the forces of modernization are contending with. Somewhere between 18% and 30% of the land in Ethiopia is owned by the Church, which pays no land taxes. The Church has a decentralized structure led by the *abune,* and some 20% of the Christian population in Ethiopia are members of the clergy. The hierarchy and clerics at the lower levels as well refuse to comply with most government directives seeking to implement programs of modernization.

Plight of Tenant Farmers

Ethiopia has been described as a feudal empire, largely because of systems of land tenure and landlord-tenant relations that still exist despite some laws to the contrary. The fact that landlord-tenant relations have not been legalized or systematised leads to an agricultural society in which, it is charged, tenants are at the mercy of their landlords. These are among the landlord-tenant practices:

Rents: Wello Province—In Wello Province, no rational norms exist for renting land. In Kalu, 44.26% of the farmers pay rent in crop, 22.95% in cash, 26.23% in crop and cash and 6.56% in undefined services. The share of the crop paid by tenants depends on whether or not oxen are supplied by the landlord. In Kalu, when oxen are supplied, 2% of the tenants pay less than 50% of their crop as rent, and 7% pay 50% or more. When oxen are not supplied, 19% of the tenants pay less than 50% as rent, and 72% pay 50% or more. These figures, compiled by the government in July 1968, indicate that 9% of the tenants in Wello receive oxen and 91% do not. Some tenants pay as much rent to landlords without being supplied with oxen as those who are supplied.

Leasing arrangements & eviction: Shoa Province—When a tenant rents land from a landlord, the agreement can be either oral or written. In Chore, only $\frac{1}{10}$ of tenants interviewed (in a 1968 government study) had written agreements with the landlords. The remaining $\frac{9}{10}$ had verbal agreements. The period of agreement was not specified in most cases. Oral agreements have no validity in court, and the written agreements include very little substance if there is no minimum period of tenant control. Written agreements usually specify only that the land may be farmed by a particular tenant. Because of the looseness of agreements, landlords may evict at will.

Extra labor services & uncompensated improvements— Tenancy conditions in various provinces include services aside from rent. These services include free labor on the farm, such as planting, threshing, fencing and the herding of cattle. In Alemaya, Harar Province, a major reason for tenants terminating their tenancy is that too many services are demanded by the landlord.

Other exploitative measures—According to a government report, a tenant who is in need of food or capital is "usually liable to agree to give up his capacity to make decisions on what crop to raise or what payments to make in order to obtain credit from the landlord." The landlord, in turn, may charge exhorbitant interest rates on the loans advanced.

It is accepted that tenants in Ethiopia have few if any rights *vis a vis* their landlords. The landlords, on the other hand, have become feudal lords with extraordinary power. The power accumulated by the landlords, which is totally independent of the government, makes the landlords a countervailing political power to the central government.

Confusing Land-Tenure Systems

In Ethiopia, there is not just one or a few land-tenure systems but a multiplicity of them. In the province of Wello, it is estimated, there are more than 111 land-tenure systems. What follows is a brief description of only a few of the variations and combinations among Ethiopia's land-tenure systems:

Muslims: Woqf lands—Muslims follow their own practices governing inheritance, even when they are settled among non-Muslims. In Chercher, Harar Province, the Shari and old Turkish laws based on Shari law apply to lands among the Muslims. *Woqf* lands are lands given by the government to the Islamic church and are under the administration of the various mosques. Total figures as to how much land the mosques in Ethiopia own do not exist. *Woqf* lands are more prevalent in some areas than in others. In Eritrea, where 40% of the population is Muslim, there are more *Woqf* lands under the authority of mosques than in Gojam, where in the town of Bahir Dar more than 90% of the population is Ethiopian Orthodox. These lands are exempt from the payment of land taxes.

Maderia land—*Maderia* land is land given by the government to an individual; it can be withdrawn at will and transferred to another person. It is granted in place of salary to government employes, and the holding is not heritable. Holders of such land refuse to pay land taxes, and the government does not force them to pay.

Galla land—*Galla* land is *maderia* land granted as pension to those who render services to the government. These landowners also do not pay land taxes.

Gebretel land—Land taken over by the government due to non-payment of land tax is called *gebretel* land. The government can lease this land to individuals for grazing and farming purposes. The defaulter has the right to reclaim the land by paying double the amount of tax due unless it has already been leased. This system leads to various complications due to the fact that often receipts for payment of tax are not given.

Government land—The emperor and his imperial family, which includes many persons beyond the biological family, own vast tracts of land. No attempt has been made to distinguish between the emperor's revenues and property and that of the state. Since the emperor's accounts are not made public, and there is no separation of state and imperial land, no knowledge exists on which to determine the amount of land owned by the state and the emperor. All that is known is that the holdings are quite large and remain tax exempt.

Gabbar land—*Gabbar* is a system of land tenure under which a person who has acquired land by purchase, grant or inheritance pays land tax to the government. It is one of the few systems of land tenure on which no tax exemption exists.

The land-tenure systems and landlord-tenant relations play an important role in the political, economic and social life of Ethiopia. They are at the root of the struggle between tradition and modernization that has shaped much of Ethiopia's recent history. An understanding of these land customs and practices is essential to make clear the problems Haile Selassie fought to overcome as he attempted to make Ethiopia a modern nation.

Wide World

Haile Selassie

MODERNIZATION & CENTRALIZATION OF
GOVERNMENT: 1930-5

New Emperor & First Constitution

Ras Tafari Makonnen was crowned Nov. 2, 1930 as Emperor Haile Selassie (Power of the Trinity) I, Conquering Lion of the Tribe of Judah, Elect of God and King of the Kings of Ethiopia.

Early in his reign the new emperor took a major step to bring the Ethiopian government into the 20th century. Traditionally, the power of the government remained in the hands of the emperor, and the crown served as a symbol of the unity of the Christian/Amhara group. In 1931, however, Haile Selassie promulgated the first Ethiopian constitution. The emperor did not relinquish power, but he did institutionalize the separation of powers.

In a speech made July 16, 1931, Haile Selassie gave his reasons for the granting of a constitution: "The constitution, which is to serve as the basis, in the future, for the maintenance of the Ethiopian government and of the laws which are based on it, and the means of applying such laws once resolved, will itself set forth the necessity of the measures suitable for ensuring its maintenance in order that this constitution of our state may remain perpetual and immutable." "Having in view the prosperity of the country, we have decided to draw up a constitution which safeguards such prosperity based on the law, and we have hope that this constitution will be a source of well-being for Ethiopia, that it will contribute to the maintenance of our government and to the happiness and prosperity of our well-beloved people, and that it will give satisfaction to all."

The first Ethiopian parliament convened 16 months later, Nov. 2, 1932.

As provided by the 1931 Constitution, 2 deliberative chambers were established, a Senate and a Chamber of Deputies. The members of the Senate were appointed by the emperor, whereas the members of the Chamber of Deputies were selected by the "nobility and the local chiefs." Neither the size of the chambers, the duration of their sessions, nor the length of the members' terms of service were specified. Active participation in the legislative process was limited. Article 34 of the constitution stated: "No law may be put forth without having been discussed by the chambers and having obtained the confirmation of the emperor." Article 6 said: "In the Ethiopian empire, supreme power rests in the hands of the emperor."

The text of the 1931 Constitution:

CHAPTER I—THE ETHIOPIAN EMPIRE & THE
SUCCESSION TO THE THRONE

Article 1. The territory of Ethiopia, in its entirety, is, from one end to the other, subject to the government of his majesty the emperor. All the natives of Ethiopia, subjects of the empire, form together the Ethiopian nation.

Article 2. The imperial government assures the union of the territory, of the nation and of the law of Ethiopia.

Article 3. The law determines that the imperial dignity shall remain perpetually attached to the line of his majesty Haile Selassie I, descendant of King Sahle Selassie, whose line descends without interruption from the dynasty of Menelik I, son of King Solomon of Jerusalem and of the Queen of Ethiopia, known as the Queen of Sheba.

Article 4. The throne and the crown of the empire shall be transmitted to the descendants of the emperor pursuant to the law of the imperial house.

Article 5. By virtue of his imperial blood, as well as by the anointing which he has received, the person of the emperor is sacred, his dignity is inviolable and his power indisputable. Consequently, he is entitled to all the honors due to him in accordance with tradition and the present constitution. The law decrees that anyone so bold as to injure the majesty of the emperor will be punished.

CHAPTER II—THE POWER & PREROGATIVES OF THE
EMPEROR

Article 6. In the Ethiopian empire supreme power rests in the hands of the emperor. He ensures the exercise thereof in conformity with the established law.

Article 7. The emperor of Ethiopia will institute the Chamber of the Senate (*Yaheg Mawossena Meker-Beth*) and the Chamber of Deputies (*Yaheg Mamria Meker-Beth*). The laws prepared by these chambers become executory by his promulgation.

Article 8. It is the emperor's right to convene the deliberative chambers and to declare the opening and the close of their sessions. He may also order their convocation before or after the usual time. He may dissolve the Chamber of Deputies.

Article 9. When the chambers are not sitting, the emperor has the right, in case of necessity, in order to maintain order and avert public dangers, to promulgate decrees taking the place of laws. The law determines that these decrees shall in due course be presented to the chambers at their first subsequent meeting, and that they shall be abrogated for the future if the chambers do not approve them.

Article 10. The emperor shall give the necessary orders to ensure the execution of the laws in force, according to the letter and the spirit thereof, and for the maintenance of public order and the development of the prosperity of the nation.

Article 11. The emperor shall lay down the organization and the regulations of all administrative departments. It is his right also to appoint and dismiss the officers of the army, as well as civil officials, and to decide as to their respective charges and salaries.

Article 12. The right of declaring war and of concluding peace is legally reserved to the emperor.

Article 13. It is the emperor's right to determine the armed forces necessary to the empire, both in time of peace and in time of war.

Article 14. The emperor has legally the right to negotiate and to sign all kinds of treaties.

Article 15. The emperor has the right to confer the title of prince and other honorific titles, to establish personal estates [and] to institute new orders.

Article 16. The emperor has the right to grant pardon, to commute penalties and to reinstate.

Article 17. If the emperor is incapable, either owing to age or sickness, of dealing with the affairs of government, a regent of the empire may be appointed, pursuant to the law of the imperial house, in order to exercise the supreme power on the emperor's behalf.

CHAPTER III—THE RIGHTS RECOGNIZED BY THE
EMPEROR AS BELONGING TO THE NATION, & THE
DUTIES INCUMBENT ON THE NATION

Article 18. The law specifies the conditions required for the status of Ethiopian subjects.

Article 19. All Ethiopian subjects, provided that they comply with the conditions laid down by law and the decrees promulgated by his majesty the emperor, may be appointed officers of the army or civil officials, or to any other posts or offices in the service of the state.

Article 20. All those who belong to the Ethiopian army owe absolute loyalty and obedience to the emperor, in conformity with the provisions of the law.

Article 21. The nation is bound to pay legal taxes.

Article 22. Within the limits provided by law, Ethiopian subjects have the right to pass freely from one place to another.

Article 23. No Ethiopian subject may be arrested, sentenced or imprisoned except in pursuance of the law.

Article 24. No Ethiopian subject may, against his will, be deprived of the right to have his case tried by the legally established court.

Article 25. Except in the cases provided by law, no domiciliary searches may be made.

Article 26. Except in the cases provided by law, no one shall have the right to violate the secrecy of the correspondence of Ethiopian subjects.

Article 27. Except in cases of public utility determined by law, no one shall be entitled to deprive an Ethiopian subject of the movable or landed property which he holds.

Article 28. All Ethiopian subjects have the right to present petitions to the government in legal form.

Article 29. The provisions of the present chapter shall in no way limit the measures which the emperor, by virtue of his supreme power, may take in the event of war or of public misfortunes menacing the interests of the nation.

CHAPTER IV—THE DELIBERATIVE CHAMBERS OF THE EMPIRE

Article 30. The deliberative chambers of the empire are the 2 following: (a) The First: Chamber of the Senate (*Yaheg Mawossena Meker-Beth*). (b) The 2d: Chamber of Deputies (*Yaheg Mamria Meker-Beth*).

Article 31. The members of the Senate shall be appointed by his majesty the emperor from among nobility (*mekuanent*) and the local chiefs (*shumoch*).

Article 32. Temporarily, and until the people are in a position to elect them themselves, the members of the Chamber of Deputies shall be chosen by the nobility (*mekuanent*) and the local chiefs (*shumoch*).

Article 33. A person who has been appointed member of the Senate may not, during the same parliamentary session, become a member of the Chamber of Deputies, and a person who has been chosen as a member of the Chamber of Deputies may not during the same parliamentary session become a member of the Senate.

Article 34. No law may be put into force without having been discussed by the chambers and having obtained the confirmation of the emperor.

Article 35. The members of the Chamber of Deputies shall be legally bound to receive and deliberate on the proposals transmitted to them by the ministers of the respective departments. However, when the deputies have an idea which could be useful to the empire or to the nation, the law reserves to them the right to communicate it to the emperor through their president, and the chamber shall deliberate on the subject if the emperor consents thereto.

Article 36. Each of the 2 chambers shall have the right to express separately to his majesty the emperor its opinion on a legislative question or on any other matter whatsoever. If the emperor does not accept its opinion, it may not, however, revert to the question during the same parliamentary session.

Article 37. The 2 chambers shall be convened annually and shall sit for ... months. If necessary, the emperor may cause them to sit longer.

Article 38. The chambers shall be convened in extraordinary session, according to requirements. In this case, it is for the emperor to fix the duration of their session.

Article 39. The opening and closing, and the duration of sessions and recesses shall be fixed identically in respect of the 2 chambers. If the Chamber of Deputies is dissolved, the Senate shall adjourn its session until later.

Article 40. If the emperor has made use of his right to dissolve the Chamber of Deputies entirely, he shall arrange for a new chamber to be assembled within 4 months.

Article 41. Neither of the 2 chambers shall commence its deliberations or undertake a debate or a vote without ⅔ of its members being present.

Article 42. If during the deliberations of the chambers the votes are equally divided, the opinion of the group to which the president of the chamber shall have adhered shall prevail.

Article 43. The president of the chamber shall state in advance whether the question forming the subject-matter of the deliberations is public or secret in character. If, after a matter has been declared secret, a member brings it to the knowledge of the public by speeches, by the press, by writings or by any other means, he shall be punished in conformity with the penal law.

Article 44. The emperor shall draw up, in the form of a law, the standing orders of the Senate and of the Chamber of Deputies.

Article 45. Except in cases of crime, judgment of which cannot be deferred, no member of the Chamber of Deputies may be prosecuted at law during the period of a parliamentary session.

Article 46. If, after deliberating an important matter, the 2 chambers come to different decisions, the emperor, having received written statements of their respective opinions, shall examine the reasons for their disagreement. After having come to a conclusion on the matter, he shall seek a compromise capable of bringing them to a final agreement, by selecting what he considers best in the 2 resolutions. In the event of its being impossible to reconcile the opinions of the 2 chambers, the emperor legally has the right either to select and promulgate the opinion of one, or to defer the question.

Article 47. The chambers may not summon ministers to their meetings even if they feel the need therefor, without having first obtained the consent of the emperor. Ministers, on their part, may not attend meetings of the chambers and take part in their deliberations without having obtained the consent of his majesty.

CHAPTER V—THE MINISTERS OF THE EMPIRE

Article 48. Ministers shall submit in writing to his majesty the emperor their opinions regarding the affairs of their respective departments; they are responsible for such opinions. Laws and decrees and all other acts emanating from the emperor in the affairs of the empire shall bear the imperial signature; subsequently the keeper of the seals (*tsafiteezaz*) shall notify them under his signature to the appropriate minister.

Article 49. When the emperor asks the opinion of his ministers on an important governmental matter, they shall deliberate together in accordance with the regulations before submitting their opinion to him.

CHAPTER VI—JURISDICTION

Article 50. Judges, sitting regularly, shall administer justice in conformity with the laws, in the name of his majesty the emperor. The organization of the courts shall be regulated by law.

Article 51. The judges shall be selected from among men having experience of judicial affairs.

Article 52. Judges shall sit in public. In cases which might affect public order or prejudice good morals, the hearing may, according to law, be held *in camera*.

Article 53. The jurisdiction of each court shall be fixed by law.

Article 54. Special courts shall judge all suits relating to administrative affairs, which are withdrawn from the jurisdiction of the other courts.

CHAPTER VII—THE BUDGET OF THE IMPERIAL GOVERNMENT

Article 55. The law determines that the receipts of the government treasury, of whatever nature they may be, shall only be expended in conformity with the annual budget fixing the sums placed at the disposal of each ministry. The annual budget shall be framed on the basis proposed by the minister of finance during the deliberations of the Chamber of Deputies and of the Senate, whose resolutions shall be submitted to the approval of his majesty the emperor.

In 1908 and 1911 Emperor Menelik II had set up a system of ministerial advisers. He had established ministries of justice, war, interior, commerce, finance, foreign affairs, agriculture, public works and posts and telegraphs under this system. In 1931 Haile Selassie institutionalized Menelik's efforts to set up a modern bureaucratic administration; he did so by establishing the existence of cabinet ministers in the constitution. (Haile Selassie also created a Ministry of Fine Arts & Education and a Ministry of Industry.) As a result, the executive government was divided between the emperor and the ministers, though the ministers were appointed by, and responsible to, the emperor. (At this time many European advisers were appointed to the various ministries.)

Haile Selassie was attempting to centralize the government, but local *rases* (princes) were trying to subvert his power. Just prior to and almost immediately after his inauguration, the emperor put down rebellions led by Ras Gugsa Wallie in Beghememder and by Ras Hailu in Gojam. Ras Hailu was condemned to death in 1932 for aiding the abortive escape from prison of ex-Emperor Lij Yasu but was later reprieved by the emperor in the sort of move, some observers hold, that Haile Selassie often takes to create loyalty to himself.

According to John Markakis and Asmelash Beyene ("Representative Institutions in Ethiopia," *The Journal of Modern African Studies,* Vol. 5, No. 2, Sept. 1967), the 1931 Constitution was aimed at eliminating gradually "the personal and arbitrary power of the [local] nobles by tightening the legal reins on its exercise. As long as the emperor retained complete control of the constitutional process of legitimation—and the constitution was designed to ensure such control—there would be no legal justification for such power." Christopher Clapham, another authority on Ethiopia, claimed in *The Institutions of the Central Ethiopian Government*** that "the 1931 Constitution had virtually no effect on the government's working, except that it established an appointed parliament."

It appears that the new parliament met infrequently, was shrouded in secrecy and was thoroughly controlled by Haile Selassie. Often, the emperor issued decrees without even presenting them to parliament for its approval.

Law in Ethiopia generally functions through customary rules of behavior. In 1930, Haile Selassie introduced a criminal code. The code was drawn up by the emperor in a further attempt to centralize the government and, additionally, to bring Ethiopia closer to the European way of doing things.

In the early 1930s Haile Selassie established some 62 administrative units throughout the country to control slavery. In an effort to upgrade the level of education, several elementary schools were opened in Addis Ababa, and about 150 Ethiopian students were sent to Europe to continue their education.

To increase the ability of the military and also to centralize its loyalty to the emperor (and shift it from the *rases*), a small military college was opened by Haile Selassie, who secured its staff from Belgium.

The first 5 years of Haile Selassie's rule show his preoccupation with the centralization of power in his own person and with the establishment of political institutions. There was little concentration on economics or finance in this period. Money was secured as needed by collecting rents from imperial land or by levying *ad hoc* "taxes" on local princes and the Ethiopian Orthodox Church. (Not until the 1940s was any currency or tax system established.) Although the Bank of Ethiopia was opened in 1931, the basic form of currency in use at this time was still the Maria Theresa thalér.

---

* An unpublished Ph.D. thesis (Oxford University, 1966)

THE ITALIAN INVASION: 1935-41

Troops of the Fascist government of Italy invaded Ethiopia Oct. 3, 1935. The capital, Addis Ababa, was captured May 5, 1936, and Haile Selassie fled to Palestine, then a British mandate. He did not return to Ethiopia until Jan. 1941.

Early Italo-Ethiopian Relations

The events culminating in the Italo-Ethiopian war go back to the 19th century. An Italian company—the Florio-Rubattine trading firm—had bought the Ethiopian Red Sea port of Assab from the local sultan in Mar. 1870, and the Italian government ultimately purchased the company's interests there in 1882. The Italians later seized the port of Beilul in Jan. 1885 and took control of the port of Massawa from Egypt in Feb. 1885. Ethiopian and Italian forces clashed at Dogali in Jan. 1887.

Just before Emperor Menelik II was crowned, he negotiated with the Italians the Treaty of Uchali (Uccialli) May 2, 1889. The Italians interpreted this treaty as giving them absolute control over the foreign affairs of Ethiopia, and they occupied Asmara. Menelik claimed that, under the treaty, Ethiopia had the right to ask for Italian advice on foreign affairs but that the treaty did not give the Italian government the power to control his nation's activities in the international area. King Humbert of Italy Jan. 1, 1890 proclaimed by royal decree the unification of all Italian possessions on the Red Sea, including Eritrea (directly bordering Ethiopia). Fearing what appeared to be an expansionist Italy, Menelik II abrogated the Treaty of Uchali in Feb. 1893.

The Italians seized Agordat Dec. 21, 1893 and Kassula July 17, 1894. In 1895 an Italian military force occupied the village of Adowa, east of Aksum, in northern Ethiopia. The Italians in 1895 also captured Adigrat in March but were forced to retreat later—at Amba Alagi Dec. 7, 1895 and at Makalle Jan. 21, 1896.

19

One of the most memorable battles in Ethiopian history—
the battle of Adowa—took place in Mar. 1896. An Ethiopian
army of about 70,000 under Menelik II soundly defeated an
Italian force of some 17,000 men. 12,000 Italians were killed in
this encounter, and most of the remaining 5,000 were captured
by the Ethiopians. This was a stunning setback for the Italians,
and it led to the Treaty of Addis Ababa, in which the Italian
government renounced the Treaty of Uchali.

Tension between the 2 countries persisted, however, and in
1900 Italy took control of Banadir (later called Italian Somaliland).

In Dec. 1925 Italy and Britain concluded an agreement in
effect accepting an Italian sphere of influence in Ethiopia. Ras
Tafari, then regent, appealed to the League of Nations June 12,
1926 against this violation of Ethiopia's rights. Italy and
Britain then asserted that they really had not intended to assign
Ethiopian economic rights to Italy.

A 20-year treaty of "perpetual friendship" was signed by
Italy and Ethiopia in Aug. 1928. The pact provided that
"neither government would under any pretext whatsoever take
any action that may prejudice or damage the independence of
the other. And both governments would submit all disputes
which could not be solved through normal diplomatic channels
by processes of conciliation and arbitration."

War Approaches

The "20-year friendship" did not last very long. Italy's
Fascist dictator, Benito Mussolini, had been asserting that
expansion in Africa was both Italy's destiny and Italy's right.
In what some observers considered an attempt to impress the
new chancellor of Germany, Adolf Hitler, Mussolini at this
time took a new look at his relations with Ethiopia. In the
spring of 1932 Mussolini sent Marshal Emilio de Bono to
Eritrea on what de Bono indicated later was a mission to see
what would have to be done to prepare for an attack on
Ethiopia. The planning apparently got under way later that
year.

In Aug. 1934 Mussolini asserted: "It is necessary to
prepare for war. Not tomorrow, but today. We are becoming
and shall become increasingly ... a military nation." This
declaration was taken as a direct reference to Ethiopia in view

of statements Mussolini had made earlier in 1934. He had said in March that "the historical objectives of Italy have 2 names: Asia and Africa.... Italy is able to introduce Africa more fully into the circle of the civilized world." He asserted that "there is no question of territorial conquest ... but of natural expansion which might lead to collaboration between Italy and Abyssinia [Ethiopia]." He warned that Italy "did not want earlier arrivals [in Africa] to block her spiritual, political and economic expansion."

Faced with what appeared to him to be an increasing threat, Haile Selassie directed his ambassador in Rome to seek a reaffirmation of the "perpetual friendship" pledged by Italy. The result was a joint Italo-Ethiopian communique, issued Sept. 28, 1934, asserting that "Italy has no intention that is not friendly toward the Ethiopian government."

The immediate pretext for Italy's Oct. 1935 invasion of Ethiopia was a relatively unimportant Ethiopian-Italian clash over a water hole. The incident had taken place 10 months previously—in Dec. 1934—in Walwal, an Ogaden watering place, on the Somaliland-Ethiopian border, to which Somali nomads brought their livestock. Italian troops and planes, with little difficulty, routed an Ethiopian unit and killed more than 100 Ethiopian soldiers. Although the incident was little different from similar clashes, Italy and the Italian press refused to let the matter drop, and observers began to suspect that Italy had decided to use the clash as a *casus belli*.

Premier Pierre Laval of France visited Mussolini in Rome in Jan. 1935 to discuss their mutual problems—in Africa and elsewhere. Laval entertained Mussolini at dinner in the French embassy Jan. 6 and is then reported to have told newsmen that he had given Mussolini "a dessert—I have given him Abyssinia." Laval later insisted in his published *Diary,* however, that "I urged Mussolini not to resort to force [in Ethiopia].... He committed the blunder of going to war. He started war against my will and despite my solemn protest."

Ethiopia, meanwhile, had referred the Walwal issue to the League of Nations Jan. 3, 1935. Laval went from Rome to Geneva, where he and Anthony Eden, then Lord Privy Seal of Britain, were instrumental in having the Walwal matter removed from the agenda of the League's Council. Instead of subjecting the issue to League action, it was decided to let the 2 disputants settle it under their friendship treaty. The arbitration procedure, however, proved fruitless.

Britain had been approached by Ethiopia for diplomatic assistance but had decided that its interests would not permit it to become involved. As Italy built up its military strength in Africa, however, Britain did undertake a mediating role. Anthony Eden went to Rome, where he presented to Mussolini June 14 an Ethiopian offer of a strip of Ogaden desert. Mussolini rejected the offer as insufficient. Britain and France in July unofficially banned the shipment of weapons to Ethiopia and warned other nations that they would consider any such shipments to Ethiopia an unfriendly act.

At about this point the Council of the League of Nations became involved in the negotiations: 3 of its members, Britain, France and Italy, took part in a series of unofficial meetings on the issue in late July and early August, and arbitration was later resumed. The report of the arbitrators, published in Sept. 1935, asserted that nobody was at fault in the Walwal incident.

The arbitration decision was rendered as Italy was completing its military mobilization and its massing of troops and supplies at home, in Eritrea and in Italian Somaliland. Mediation efforts by the League of Nations and proffered concessions by Ethiopia proved unavailing. Mussolini reportedly told his cabinet that he intended "to wipe out the defeat which the Ethiopians inflicted on Italy 39 years ago at Adowa and dictate terms of peace to the emperor." He was quoted as saying: "With the League, without the League, against the League, the problem has only one solution. We will shoot straight."

Most observers agreed that in what was its first major test, the League had failed: Italy's intentions in regard to Ethiopia had been no secret. Ethiopia had called for help—repeatedly. But help had not come.

Italy Attacks

Mussolini announced Oct. 2, 1935 that his decision was war. Italians massed in their public squares that afternoon. In a broadcast to his awaiting countrymen *il Duce* said:

Black Shirts of the revolution! Men and women of all Italy! Italians scattered throughout the world, over the hills and beyond the seas: Hear me!

A solemn hour is about to strike in the history of our country. 20 million people fill, at this moment, all the squares of Italy.... 20 million people, with one heart, one will, one decision alone. This manifestation ought to show the world that Italy and Fascism are a single entity, perfect, absolute, unalterable. Only crass idiots, ignorant of Italy in 1935, the 13th year of the Facist era, could believe otherwise.

For many months the wheel of destiny, under the impulse of our calm determination, has been moving toward its goal; now its rhythm is faster and can no longer be stopped. Here is not just an army marching toward a military objective but a whole people, 44 million souls, against whom the blackest of all injustices has been committed—that of denying them a place in the sun. When in 1915 Italy mixed her fate with that of the Allies—how much praise there was from them, how many promises! But after a common victory, which cost Italy 670,000 dead, 400,000 mutilated, and a million wounded, at the peace table these same Allies withheld from Italy all but a few crumbs of the rich colonial loot.... We have waited patiently for redress in Ethiopia for 40 years. Now—enough!

At the League of Nations, instead of recognizing this, there is talk of sanctions. Until I am proved wrong, I refuse to believe that France ... or the people of Great Britain, with whom we have never quarreled, would risk throwing Europe into catastrophe to defend a country in Africa well known to be without the least shade of civilization. To economic sanctions we will reply with our discipline, our sobriety, our spirit of sacrifice!

To military sanctions we shall reply with military measures! To acts of war we shall reply with acts of war!

But let it be said at the start, in the most categorical way, that we will do everything possible to avoid this colonial conflict flaring up into a European war. But never, as in this historical epoch, has the Italian people shown so well the quality of its spirit and the strength of its character. And it is against this people, people of poets, of saints, navigators, that they dare to speak of sanctions. Proletarian and Fascist Italy ... on your feet!

Within hours Italian forces were on the march. They had been waiting, in some cases for months, and Mussolini Sept. 29 had set the day and hour for hostilities to start. In his Sept. 29 message he had said: "I order you to begin advance early on the 3d. I say the 3d of October."

Italian troops crossed the Mareb River from Eritrea Oct. 3 and advanced into Ethiopia. The attack on Haile Selassie's kingdom had begun.

In Addis Ababa the chiefs of the nation had been called into assembly in the courtyard of the emperor's palace Oct. 3, and the grand chamberlain read to the chiefs this royal proclamation intended for the entire nation:

The conflict between Italy and our country ... started at Walwal on 5 Dec. 1934. Our soldiers ... were attacked, in our territory.... Italy demanded reparations and apologies.... When, after much resistance on Italy's part, we were able, thanks to our perseverance and the effects of the League of Nations Council, to bring this difference before the arbitrators, they unanimously recognized that we were guiltless of the fault Italy imputed to us. But Italy, which for a long time has shown an unconcealed desire to acquire our country, now prepares to attack us.... The hour is grave. Arise, each of you. Take up arms, and rush to the defense of your country. Rally to your chiefs; obey them with single purpose, and repel the invader. May those who are unable because of weakness and infirmity to take an active part in this sacred quarrel, help us with their prayers. The opinion of the world has been revolted by this aggression against us. God be with us all. All forward for your emperor and for your country!

Haile Selassie then appeared at a window above the court-yard. As drums relayed mobilization orders throughout the country, the emperor said: "Do not be afraid. I shall be with you in battle. Do not be afraid of death. You will be dying for your country. March on to death or victory. Let all take up their arms, stand up and move on at the call of your country. The world is with us, God is on our side. March on for emperor and country."

Haile Selassie and his military aides had obviously foreseen the impending attack, but their attempts to prepare for it appeared to be both belated and insufficient. The Ethiopian regular army numbered perhaps 100,000 men. But modern arms were expensive and hard to get, even after the British-French embargo was lifted. The terrain, the nature of Ethiopia's regular and irregular forces, the type of armaments available to the Ethiopians and the nature of their enemy—a well-equipped, modern force with 400 warplanes—dictated Ethiopia's dependence on guerrilla strategy.

Ethiopia again asked for action from the League of Nations, and a committee of 6 (Britain, Chile, Denmark, France, Portugal and Rumania) was set up Oct. 5 to get the facts. The committee, directed to report by Oct. 7, informed the League's Council of its conclusion that "the Italian government has resorted to war in disregard of its covenants under Article 12 of the covenant of the League of Nations." The League's Assembly then met Oct. 11 and voted, 50 to 4 (Austria, Hungary, Italy and Albania opposed), to condemn Italy for this illegal act of war.

The problem of coordinated action—including sanctions—was the next matter, and a subcommittee of 18 was created by the League to see what should be done. The League accepted these 4 proposals drawn up by the committee: (1) The arms embargo against Ethiopia was lifted; (2) the Italian government was to receive no more foreign credits, and financial transactions with Italy were to be canceled; (3) League members agreed to import nothing from Italy (except gold, silver and coin), and (4) League members were to halt many of their normal exports to Italy. On Britain's insistance, however, the export ban deliberately omitted such war-making essentials as coal, oil, iron and steel—and the sanctions were therefore seen as meaningless as a means of discouraging aggression.

Among League nations, only Albania, Austria, Hungary and Paraguay refused to apply sanctions. The U.S., not a member of the League, avoided any definite action either favoring or approving the sanctions. Observers noted that while the U.S. embargoed non-essential arms to Italy, the U.S. continued to ship really vital war-making items to the Italians.

The Italian attack on Ethiopia was begun under the command of Marshal Emilio de Bono, but within 2 months he was replaced by the more enterprising Marshal Pietro Badoglio, under whose orders most major sections of Ethiopia were eventually brought under Italian control. As the Italian forces fought their way toward Addis Ababa, Haile Selassie and his imperial family left the capital May 2, 1936 to go into exile. Badoglio entered Addis Ababa May 5, and Mussolini announced from his balcony in Rome: "The war is over. Ethiopia is Italian."

According to Italian data, the conquest of Ethiopia cost 1,757 Italian and 1,593 Eritrean lives. The Ethiopian government reported (in 1946) that 275,000 Ethiopian troops were killed in action, an additional 78,500 "patriots" killed during the later struggle against the 5-year occupation, 17,800 women and children killed by bombing, and 30,000 slain in a "massacre of Feb. 1937." 35,000 Ethiopians were reported to have died in concentration camps; 24,000 were executed by the occupiers, and 300,000 reportedly died of privations caused by the war's destruction. The cost to Ethiopia was thus given as a total of 760,300 lives.

Haile Selassie Before the League of Nations

Haile Selassie rose to world prominence June 30, 1936 when the short, thin emperor appeared before the Assembly of the League of Nations in Geneva, Switzerland to plead his country's cause. The special Assembly session had been called to hear Ethiopia's complaint against Italy. Haile Selassie came to

Geneva after discussing his country's troubles with Anthony Eden in London.

In his speech—one of the major addresses of the decade and one of the most important heard by the League—Haile Selassie reviewed the recent history of Italo-Ethiopian relations and called into question the entire principle of collective security. The intense but dignified emperor warned the League that if it did not act against Italy, the very existence of collective security and of the League itself was at stake. "The confidence that each state is to place in international treaties" was also at stake, he declared. He told the world's representatives that the Italian forces had made war on Ethiopian civilians as well as on soldiers and had used poison gas against his people.

The text of Haile Selassie's address to the League of Nations (translated from Amharic):

I, Haile Selassie I, emperor of Ethiopia, am here today to claim that justice which is due to my people, and the assistance promised to it 8 months ago, when 50 nations asserted that aggression had been committed in violation of international treaties.

There is no precedent for a head of state himself speaking in this Assembly. But there is also no precedent for a people being victim of such injustice and being at present threatened by abandonment to its aggressor. Also, there has never before been an example by any government proceeding to the systematic extermination of a nation by barbarous means, in violation of the most solemn promises made by the nations of the earth that there should not be used against innocent human beings the terrible poison of harmful gases. It is to defend a people struggling for its age-old independence that the head of the Ethiopian empire has come to Geneva to fulfil this supreme duty, after having himself fought at the head of his armies.

I pray to Almighty God that He may spare nations the terrible sufferings that have just been inflicted on my people and of which the chiefs who accompany me here have been the horrified witnesses. It is my duty to inform the governments assembled in Geneva, responsible as they are for the lives of millions of men, women and children, of the deadly peril which threatens them, by describing to them the fate which has been suffered by Ethiopia.

It is not only upon warriors that the Italian government has made war. It has above all attacked populations far removed from hostilities, in order to terrorize and exterminate them.

At the beginning, towards the end of 1935, Italian aircraft hurled upon my armies bombs of tear-gas. Their effects were but slight. The soldiers learned to scatter, waiting until the wind had rapidly dispersed the poisonous gases. The Italian aircraft then resorted to mustard gas. Barrels of liquid were hurled upon armed groups. But this means also was not effective; the liquid affected only a few soldiers, and barrels upon the ground were themselves a warning to troops and to the population of the danger.

It was at the time when the operations for the encircling of Makalle [in northern Ethiopia] were taking place that the Italian command, fearing a rout, followed the procedure which it is now my duty to denounce to the world. Special sprayers were installed on board aircraft so that they could vaporize, over vast areas of territory, a fine, death-dealing rain. Groups of 9, 15, 18 aircraft followed one another so that the fog issuing from them formed a continuous sheet. It was thus that, as from the end of Jan. 1936, soldiers, women, children, cattle, rivers, lakes and pastures were drenched continually with this deadly rain. In order to kill off systematically all living creatures, in order the more surely to poison waters and pastures, the Italian command made its aircraft pass over and over again. That was its chief method of warfare.

The very refinement of barbarism consisted in carrying ravage and terror into the most densely populated parts of the territory, the points farthest removed from the scene of hostilities. The object was to scatter fear and death over a great part of the Ethiopian territory.

These fearful tactics succeeded. Men and animals succumbed. The deadly rain that fell from the aircraft made all those whom it touched fly shrieking with pain. All those who drank the poisoned water or ate the infected food also succumbed in dreadful suffering. In tens of thousands, the victims of the Italian mustard gas fell. It is in order to denounce to the civilized world the tortures inflicted upon the Ethiopian people that I resolved to come to Geneva.

None other than myself and my brave companions in arms could bring the League of Nations the undeniable proof. The appeals of my delegates addressed to the League of Nations had remained without any answer; my delegates had not been witnesses. That is why I decided to come myself to bear witness against the crime perpetrated against my people and give Europe a warning of the doom that awaits it, if it should bow before the accomplished fact.

Is it necessary to remind the Assembly of the various stages of the Ethiopian drama? For 20 years past, either as heir apparent, regent of the empire or as emperor, I have never ceased to use all my efforts to bring my country the benefits of civilization, and in particular to establish relations of good neighborliness with adjacent powers. In particular I succeeded in concluding with Italy the Treaty of Friendship of 1928, which absolutely prohibited the resort, under any pretext whatsoever, to force of arms, substituting for force and pressure the conciliation and arbitration on which civilized nations have based international order.

In its report of Oct. 5, 1935, the Committee of 13 [of the League] recognized my effort and the results that I had achieved. The governments thought that the entry of Ethiopia into the League, whilst giving that country a new guarantee for the maintenance of her territorial integrity and independence, would help her to reach a higher level of civilization. It does not seem that in Ethiopia today there is more disorder and insecurity than in 1923. On the contrary, the country is more united and the central power is better obeyed.

I should have procured still greater results for my people if obstacles of every kind had not been put in the way by the Italian government, the government which stirred up revolt and armed the rebels. Indeed the Rome government, as it has today openly proclaimed, has never ceased to prepare for the conquest of Ethiopia. The treaties of friendship it signed with me were not sincere; their only object was to hide its real intention from me. The Italian government asserts that for 14 years it has been preparing for its present conquest. It therefore recognizes today that when it supported the admission of Ethiopia to the League of Nations in 1923, when it concluded the Treaty of Friendship in 1928, when it signed the pact of Paris outlawing war, it was deceiving the whole world.

The Ethiopian government was, in these solemn treaties, given additional guarantees of security which would enable it to achieve further progress along the pacific path of reform on which it had set its feet and to which it was devoting all its strength and all its heart.

The Walwal incident, in Dec. 1934, came as a thunderbolt to me. The Italian provocation was obvious, and I did not hesitate to appeal to the League of Nations. I invoked the provisions of the treaty of 1928, the principles of the covenant [of the League]; I urged the procedure of conciliation and arbitration.

Unhappily for Ethiopia, this was the time when a certain government [Britain] considered that the European situation made it imperative at all costs to obtain the friendship of Italy. The price paid was the abandonment of Ethiopian independence to the greed of the Italian government. This secret agreement [of Jan. 1935, between Britain and Italy, recognizing Italian influence over Ethiopia], contrary to the obligations of the covenant, has exerted a great influence over the course of events. Ethiopia and the whole world have suffered and are still suffering today its disastrous consequences.

This first violation of the covenant was followed by many others. Feeling itself encouraged in its policy against Ethiopia, the Rome government feverishly made war preparations, thinking that the concerted pressure which was beginning to be exerted on the Ethiopian government might perhaps not overcome the resistance of my people to Italian domination.

The time had to come, thus all sorts of difficulties were placed in the way with a view to breaking up the procedure of conciliation and arbitration. All kinds of obstacles were placed in the way of that procedure. Governments tried to prevent the Ethiopian government from finding arbitrators amongst their nationals: when once the arbitral tribunal was set up, pressure was exercised so that an award favorable to Italy should be given. All this was in vain: the arbitrators—2 of whom were Italian officials—were forced to recognize unanimously that in the Walwal incident, as in the subsequent incidents, no international responsibility was to be attributed to Ethiopia.

Following on this award, the Ethiopian government sincerely thought that an era of friendly relations might be opened with Italy. I loyally offered my hand to the Rome government.

The Assembly was informed by the report of the Committee of 13, dated Oct. 5, 1935, of the details of the events which occurred after the month of Dec. 1934 and up to Oct. 3, 1935. It will be sufficient if I quote a few of the conclusions of that report (Nos. 24, 25 and 26): The Italian memorandum (containing the complaints made by Italy) was laid on the council table on Sept. 4, 1935, whereas Ethiopia's first appeal to the council had been made on Dec. 14, 1934. In the interval between these 2 dates, the Italian government opposed the consideration of the question by the council on the ground that the only appropriate procedure was that provided for in the Italo-Ethiopian Treaty of 1928. Throughout the whole of that period, moreover, the dispatch of Italian troops to East Africa was proceeding. These shipments of troops were represented to the council by the Italian government as necessary for the defense of its colonies menaced by Ethiopia's preparations. Ethiopia, on the contrary, drew attention to the official pronouncements made in Italy which, in its opinion, left no doubt "as to the hostile intentions of the Italian government."

From the outset of the dispute, the Ethiopian government has sought a settlement by peaceful means. It has appealed to the procedures of the covenant. The Italian government, desiring to keep strictly to the procedures of the Italo-Ethiopian Treaty of 1928, the Ethiopian government assented. It invariably stated that it would faithfully carry out the arbitral award oven if the decision went against it. It agreed that the question of the ownership of Walwal should not be dealt with by the arbitrators, because the Italian government would not agree to such a course. It asked the council to dispatch neutral observers and offered to lend itself to any inquiries upon which the council might decide.

Once the Walwal dispute had been settled by arbitration, however, the Italian government submitted its detailed memorandum to the council in support of its claim to liberty of action. It asserted that a case like that of Ethiopia cannot be settled by the means provided by the covenant. It stated that, "since this question affects vital interest and is of primary importance to Italian security and civilization," it "would be failing in its most elementary duty, did it not cease once and for all to place any confidence in Ethiopia, reserving full liberty to adopt any measures that may become necessary to ensure the safety of its colonies and to safeguard its own interests."

Those are the terms of the report of the Committee of 13. The council and the Assembly unanimously adopted the conclusion that the Italian government had violated the covenant and was in a state of aggression.

I did not hesitate to declare that I did not wish for war, that it was imposed upon me, and I should struggle solely for the independence and integrity of my people, and that in that struggle I was the defender of the cause of all small states exposed to the greed of a powerful neighbor.

In Oct. 1935 the 52 nations who are listening to me today gave me an assurance that the aggressor would not triumph, that the resources of the covenant would be employed in order to ensure the reign of right and the failure of violence. I ask the 52 nations not to forget today the policy upon which they embarked 8 months ago, and on faith of which I directed the resistance of my people against the aggressor whom they had denounced to the world. Despite the inferiority of my weapons, the complete lack of aircraft, artillery, munitions, hospital services, my confidence in the League was absolute. I thought it to be impossible that 52 nations, including the most powerful in the world, should be successfully opposed by a single aggressor. Counting on the faith due to treaties, I had made no preparation for war, and that is the case with certain small countries in Europe.

When the danger became more urgent, being aware of my responsibilities towards my people, during the first 6 months of 1935 I tried to acquire armaments. Many governments proclaimed an embargo to prevent my doing so, whereas the Italian government, through the Suez Canal, was given all facilities for transporting, without cessation and without protest, troops, arms and munitions.

On Oct. 3, 1935, the Italian troops invaded my territory. A few hours later only I decreed general mobilization. In my desire to maintain peace I had, following the example of a great country in Europe on the eve of the Great War, caused my troops to withdraw 30 kilometers so as to remove any pretext of provocation.

War then took place in the atrocious conditions which I have laid before the Assembly. In that unequal struggle between a government commanding more than 42 million inhabitants, having at its disposal financial, industrial and technical means which enabled it to create unlimited quantities of the most death-dealing weapons, and, on the other hand, a small people of 12 million inhabitants, without arms, without resources, having on its side only the justice of its own cause and the promise of the League of Nations, what real assistance was given to Ethiopia by the 52 nations who had declared the Rome government guilty of a breach of the covenant and had undertaken to prevent the triumph of the aggressor? Has each of the states members, as it was its duty to do in virtue of its signature appended to Article 15 of the covenant, considered the aggressor as having committed an act of war personally directed against itself? I had placed all my hopes in the execution of these undertakings. My confidence had been confirmed by the repeated declarations made in the council to the effect that aggression must not be rewarded, and that force would end by being compelled to bow before right.

In Dec. 1935, the council made it quite clear that its feelings were in harmony with those of hundreds of millions of people who, in all parts of the world, had protested against the proposal to dismember Ethiopia. It was constantly repeated that there was not merely a conflict between the Italian government and the League of Nations, and that is why I personally refused all proposals to my personal advantage made to me by the Italian government, if only I would betray my people and the covenant of the League of Nations. I was defending the cause of all small peoples who are threatened with aggression.

What have become of the promises made to me as long ago as Oct. 1935? I noted with grief, but without surprise, that 3 powers considered their undertakings under the covenant as absolutely of no value. Their connections with Italy impelled them to refuse to take any measures whatsoever in order to stop Italian aggression. On the contrary, it was a profound disappointment to me to learn the attitude of a certain government [Britain], which, whilst ever protesting its scrupulous attachment to the covenant, has tirelessly used all its efforts to prevent its observance. As soon as any measure which was likely to be rapidly effective was proposed, various pretexts were devised in order to postpone even consideration of the measure. Did the secret agreements of Jan. 1935 provide for this tireless obstruction?

The Ethiopian government never expected other governments to shed their soldiers' blood to defend the covenant when their own immediately personal interests were not at stake. Ethiopian warriors asked only for means to defend themselves. On many occasions I have asked for financial assistance for the purchase of arms. That assistance has been constantly refused me. What, then, in practice, is the meaning of Article 16 of the covenant and of collective security?

The Ethiopian government's use of the railway from Djibouti to Addis Ababa was in practice hampered as regards transport of arms intended for the Ethiopian forces. At the present moment this is the chief, if not the only, means of supply of the Italian armies of occupation. The rules of neutrality should have prohibited transports intended for Italian forces, but there is not even neutrality since Article 16 lays upon every state member of the League the duty not to remain a neutral but to come to the aid not of the aggressor but of the victim of aggression. Has the covenant been respected? Is it today being respected?

Finally a statement has just been made in their parliaments by the governments of certain powers, amongst them the most influential members of the League of Nations, that since the aggressor has succeeded in occupying a large part of Ethiopian territory, they propose not to continue the application of any economic and financial measures that may have been decided upon against the Italian government.

These are the circumstances in which at the request of the Argentine government, the Assembly of the League of Nations meets to consider the situation created by Italian aggression.

I assert that the problem submitted to the Assembly today is a much wider one. It is not merely a question of the settlement of Italian aggression. It is collective security: it is the very existence of the League of Nations. It is the confidence that each state is to place in international treaties. It is the value of promises made to small states that their integrity and their independence shall be respected and ensured. It is the principle of the equality of states on the one hand, or otherwise the obligation laid upon small powers to accept the bonds of vassalship. In a word, it is international morality that is at stake. Have the signatures appended to a treaty value only in so far as the signatory powers have a personal, direct and immediate interest involved?

No subtlety can change the problem or shift the grounds of the discussion. It is in all sincerity that I submit these considerations to the Assembly. At a time when my people are threatened with extermination, when the support of the League may ward off the final blow, may I be allowed to speak with complete frankness, without reticence, in all directness such as is demanded by the rule of equality as between all states members of the League?

Apart from the Kingdom of the Lord, there is not on this earth any nation that is superior to any other. Should it happen that a strong government finds it may with impunity destroy a weak people, then the hour strikes for that weak people to appeal to the League of Nations to give its judgment in all freedom. God and history will remember your judgment.

I have heard it asserted that the inadequate sanctions already applied have not achieved their object. At no time, and under no circumstances, could sanctions that were intentionally inadequate, intentionally badly applied, stop an aggressor. This is not a case of the impossibility of stopping an aggressor but of the refusal to stop an aggressor. When Ethiopia requested and requests that she should be given financial assistance, was that a measure which it was impossible to apply whereas financial assistance of the League has been granted, even in times of peace, to 2 countries and exactly to 2 countries who have refused to apply sanctions against the aggressor?

Faced by numerous violations by the Italian government of all international treaties that prohibit resort to arms and the use of barbarous methods of warfare, it is my painful duty to note that the initiative has today been taken with a view to raising sanctions. Does this initiative not mean in practice the abandonment of Ethiopia to the aggressor? On the very eve of the day when I was about to attempt a supreme effort in the defense of my people before this Assembly, does not this initiative deprive Ethiopia of one of her last chances to succeed in obtaining the support and guarantee of states members? Is that the guidance the League of Nations and each of the states members are entitled to expect from the great powers when they assert their right and their duty to guide the action of the League?

Placed by the aggressor face to face with the accomplished fact, are states going to set up the terrible precedent of bowing before force?

Your Assembly will doubtless have laid before it proposals for the reform of the covenant and for rendering more effective the guarantee of collective security. Is it the covenant that needs reform? What undertakings can have any value if the will to keep them is lacking? It is international morality which is at stake and not the articles of the covenant.

On behalf of the Ethiopian people, a member of the League of Nations, I request the Assembly to take all measures proper to ensure respect for the covenant. I renew my protest against the violations of treaties of which the Ethiopian people has been the victim. I declare in the face of the whole world that the emperor, the government and the people of Ethiopia will not bow before force; that they maintain their claims that they will use all means in their power to ensure the triumph of right and the respect of the covenant.

I ask the 52 nations, who have given the Ethiopian people a promise to help them in their resistance to the aggressor, what are they willing to do for Ethiopia? And the great powers who have promised the guarantee of collective security to small states on whom weighs the threat that they may one day suffer the fate of Ethiopia, I ask what measures do you intend to take?

Representatives of the world, I have come to Geneva to discharge in your midst the most painful of the duties of the head of a state. What reply shall I have to take back to my people?

The only reply came July 4, a few days after Haile Selassie's speech, when the League of Nations voted to call off its sanctions against Italy. The emperor had failed to rally the League on Ethiopia's behalf, and the League had failed to secure its own future. Haile Selassie went to England, where he remained in exile until 1940.

Occupation by Italy

The Italian occupation of Ethiopia met with considerable resistance, although many wealthy landed Ethiopians rallied to the Italian cause in the hope of reestablishing their regional power bases, which Haile Selassie had attempted to limit through his policy of political centralization. The Italian military force under the command of Marshal Pietro Badoglio was hindered continually and seriously by loosely organized guerrilla resistance groups. (One such group, the Black Lions, was made up largely of educated Ethiopians.)

In Feb. 1937 the viceroy in Ethiopia, Marshal Rodolfo Graziani, was wounded in an unsuccessful assassination attempt by 2 Ethiopians, Abraha Deboch and Mogas Asgadom. The Italians retaliated by killing thousands of unarmed Ethiopians, including several hundred educated ones. The deaths of the latter were an especially severe blow to an Ethiopia that had few educated citizens.

The Italians also attempted to reduce the power of the Ethiopian Orthodox Church, and in 1937, the invaders killed hundreds of monks at the monastery of Debra Libanos. In addition many churches were burned throughout the country.

By early 1938 it appeared evident that the occupation had failed since no real control over the Ethiopians had been achieved. Marshal Graziani was replaced as viceroy by the Duke of Aosta. A large network of roads was built in northern Ethiopia, and many buildings were constructed in Addis Ababa. The resistance, however, continued. Even by 1940 Italy had little to show in Ethiopia. No money could be collected from the peasantry in Ethiopia, and the occupation was costing Italy a fortune.

Haile Selassie went July 2, 1940 to Khartoum, Sudan, where the British, Sudanese and a small Ethiopian force were planning an attack on the Italians in Ethiopia. This joint force entered Ethiopia in Jan. 1941, and the Italians retreated. Haile Selassie, once again upon Ethiopian soil, expressed his gratitude to the Sudan and Britain Jan. 22, 1941 for their aid in liberating Ethiopia from Italy. The Italian retreat continued and eventually became a rout.

Haile Selassie reentered Addis Ababa May 5, 1941, and the war was virtually over. According to the emperor, 130,000 Italians had been captured. In his victory day speech of May 5, 1941, Haile Selassie condemned the Italian invaders for their atrocities, praised the Ethiopian resistance and asked his people not to engage in retribution against the Italians. This address, made from the palace balcony, came to be known as the "Great Mercy Proclamation." In it the emperor said:

> This day is a day on which a fresh chapter of this history of "new Ethiopia" begins. If we desire to be reminiscent of the affliction which befell Ethiopia during the past years we shall speak only of her recent history. When Ethiopia ... was attacked in ... [1896] by Italy ... with the intention of destroying her freedom, her brave sons fought at Adowa, and she saved her independence. The Treaty of Uchali in 1889 was not the only cause of the battle fought at Adowa. It was only a pretext for the constant desire that Italy had had of ruling Ethiopia.... When Italy began a war of aggression on Ethiopia ... we went against her.... But as it was apparent she was bent on exterminating our people ... we went to appeal to the League of Nations to claim justice.... How many are the young men, and women, the priests and the monks whom the Italians pitilessly massacred! ... The blood and bones of those who were killed with spades and pickaxes, of those ... hammered to death ..., clubbed ..., stoned ..., burned alive ..., perished of hunger ... have been crying for justice. But ... today is a day on which Ethiopia is stretching her hands to God in joy and thankfulness ..., a day of rejoicing for us all. Therefore let us rejoice ... in the spirit of Christ. Do not return evil for evil. Do not indulge in atrocities.... Take care not to spoil the good name of Ethiopia by acts which are worthy of the enemy.

Many Italians, in fact, remained in Ethiopia after the war to engage in business and commerce. As middle class businessmen, they eventually became vital to the economy of Ethiopia, and many of them still live throughout Ethiopia.

The Italian-Ethiopian war had at least 2 major implications: Ethiopia was the first battle arena of fascism. Shortly after the beginning of the fighting in Ethiopia, the Spanish Civil War erupted, and in 1936 Hitler's Germany occupied the Rhineland. In effect, Ethiopia was the first major battlefield of World War II. And secondly, the failure of the League of Nations to invoke meaningful collective security against Italy was the beginning of the end for the League. For the League was largely predicated on the principle of collective security, and when the League abandoned this principle in Ethiopia, it destroyed faith in its future.

RESTORATION & CONTINUITY: 1942-9

British Predominance

Early in 1942, Britain, mired down in the struggle against Germany, forced Haile Selassie to accept certain demands. These demands, incorporated in the Anglo-Ethiopian Agreement of Jan. 31, 1942, provided that: (1) Britain's diplomatic representative to Ethiopia "shall take precedence over any other foreign representative accredited to his imperial majesty"; (2) British advisers would serve the Ethiopian administration, and no additional advisers were to be appointed except with British consent; (3) British military tribunals would try all enemy war-crime suspects; (4) Ethiopia would enact laws against trading with the Axis powers (Germany, Italy and Japan); (5) British aircraft would be permitted free access throughout Ethiopia, and (6) in return for the rights acquired by Britain, the British would pay Ethiopia £ 2½ million.

This British predominance lasted for nearly 3 years. Then, because of changed military circumstances in Europe in 1944, the treaty of 1942 was superseded by an Anglo-Ethiopian Agreement of Dec. 19, 1944. Under the 1944 agreement, Ethiopia was permitted to appoint British advisers as the Ethiopian government "sees fit." The discretion was transferred to the Ethiopian government from the British. In addition, jurisdiction over British subjects was to be exercised by Ethiopian courts, and the British government relinquished control of the Franco-Ethiopian railway running from Addis Ababa to Djibouti. The agreement provided for the establishment of a British military mission to Ethiopia, and until the termination of the agreement, the British military was permitted to administer the Ogaden region of Harar province.

The 1944 agreement ended in 1945, and full sovereignty was restored to Ethiopia by the British.

Economic & Modernization Programs Resumed

Despite the British presence, Haile Selassie quickly reestablished his policy of political and administrative centralization and modernization. This was a major goal of his activities in the period 1942-9. Haile Selassie's modernization program and his efforts to centralize authority were fought consistently by the 2 main forces whose power was threatened—the local nobles and the Church.

The emperor also put added stress on economic improvement. Some of the major legislation of the early 1940s dealt with the financial situation of Ethiopia, and an official government gazette, the *Negarit Gazeta,* was introduced Mar. 10, 1942 for promulgating and announcing legislation.

Haile Selassie Aug. 26, 1942 established a State Bank of Ethiopia, and 7 directors were chosen to administer it. A government-owned airline, Ethiopian Airlines, began operation in Dec. 1946 under the management of Trans-World Airlines. The latter, a U.S. company, agreed to train Ethiopian personnel to run the airline.

Although Haile Selassie had ordered the freeing of the slaves of Ethiopia in 1924, some Ethiopians continued the illegal practice. The emperor Aug. 26, 1942, therefore, issued a new Proclamation outlawing slavery. It specified prison sentences and fines for those who continued to keep slaves.

The 1942 & 1944 Land Tax Measures

Among the major economic reforms undertaken were efforts to modernize the system of land taxation. Under Proclamation* No. 8 of Mar. 30, 1942, land taxes were levied throughout Ethiopia to obtain revenues to help stabilize the government. All land was divided into 3 categories: fertile, semi-fertile and poor. For each *gasha* (40 hectares) of fertile land, a tax of E$15 was levied (US$1 = E$2.50); for semi-fertile land E$10 was charged, and for poor land E$5. The interior minister was empowered to make rules providing for the measurement and classification of land. The proclamation

---

* Proclamations are laws issued by the emperor without recourse to parliament.

implied that no great diversity in land tenure existed and that the universal standards demanded by the law would be applied equitably throughout the state. It ordered that "every land-owner shall be liable to pay tax at the rates specified."

2 years later, in Proclamation No. 70 of Sept. 11, 1944, the government took note of some of the difficulties and deter-mined that the "system of land taxation should be revised." The first major change instituted in Proclamation No. 70 of 1944 was the explicit reference made to the provinces of Ethiopia. Gojam, Tigre and Beghemder were excluded from such standards as (a) a land tax payable as charged in the 1942 Proclamation and (b) a tithe, traditionally paid in kind and henceforth to be paid in dollars. The rates for the tithe on land were E\$35 per *gasha* of fertile land, E\$30 per *gasha* of semi-fertile land and E\$10 per *gasha* of poor land. The 3 provinces were excluded because of the system of communal land tenure prevalent in these areas.

Of all the systems of land tenure in Ethiopia, one of the most troublesome, insofar as taxation is concerned, is the communal system. This system exists throughout most of Gojam Province and is prevalent in Tigre and Beghemder. According to Allen Hoben in *The Role of Ambilineal Descent Groups in Gojam Amhara Social Organization,** the communal land system is "very simple and derives entirely from one principle. This principle is that the land of a parent is divided equally among all of his or her biological children (without regard to seniority or sex)." This division of land, however, relates to usage rights rather than to ownership, since theoreti-cally the land is owned by the family founder.

According to H. S. Mann and J. C. D. Lawrence†, the problem insofar as tax laws and tax collection are concerned is the fact that "in Gojam, where land is held communally by members of an extended family, only the name of the family founder, who may have died hundreds of years ago, is entered [on the tax register], and there is no record at all of present day owners." Thus, in a majority of cases, the tax register contains

---

* An unpublished Ph.D. thesis (University of California, Berkeley, 1963)

†In *FAO Land Policy Project (Ethiopia):* "Land Registration in Ethiopia" (1964)

few details as to who actually owns or farms the land. In fact, the fear of communal land inhabitants in having any new tax law passed, or any land survey conducted, and their success in preventing any real application of such is shown in the following figures (for the 3 communal land provinces) on the percentage of land measured since 1943 (as of 1964):

	Estimated Total Land Area (Sq. Km.)	Area Measured Since 1943 (Sq. Km.)	Percent of Total Land Area Measured
Gojam	61,000	49	.1
Beghemder	78,200	0	—
Tigre	67,000	1,419	2.0

Even if the government had learned the names of individuals owning or farming land in communal areas, it would have been impossible, because of the lack of measured boundaries, to determine how much should be paid in land taxes. These farmers, therefore, prevented the government from learning anything that would allow any forceful application of land taxes. After the 1942 Land Tax Proclamation was issued, many farmers in Gojam Province forcibly stopped any measurement from taking place and prevented tax collectors from setting foot on their land. Although there is little knowledge as to what took place during 1942-4, it is known that the Ethiopian government felt compelled to make concessions to Gojam and, therefore, revised the 1942 document.

In addition to granting concessions to the 3 communal land areas, the Land Tax Proclamation of 1944 allowed additional exemptions from the land tax. Excused from payment were holders of *rist-gult, siso-gult* and *samon.* Both *siso-gult* and *rist-gult,* as explained by Gebre-Wold Ingida Worq in "Ethiopia's Traditional System of Land Tenure and Taxation" (*Ethiopia Observer,* Vol. V, No. 4, 1962), were traditional exemptions under which "the government allocated to the first tiller of the soil a quarter or a third or even more of the land which he had cultivated." This meant that the original landowner was not liable for paying a land tax. *Samon* refers to Coptic Church lands. Additional rules applying to these exemption holders:

Rist-gult—The person having *rist-gult* was entitled to collect land tax from the landowners settled on the land at rates prescribed by law, *i.e.,* E$15, E$10 and E$5 per *gasha* of fertile, semi-fertile and poor land, respectively. Out of the land tax collected, he paid to the government treasury at a uniform rate of E$3.50 per gasha for all classes of land and kept the rest.

According to a 1968 government report, "the rights of *rist-gult* have been granted to the emperor ..., to members of the royal family and to some people as reward for their meritorious service." The royal land grant of *rist-gult* is one of the most traditional of land tenure systems; it extends to the Middle Ages and beyond.

Although the rates of *rist-gult* were prescribed by law, it has been traditionally accepted that the holders of *rist-gult* can collect as much as possible. Figures on the number of individuals exempt from land tax payments because of *rist-gult* do not exist, but according to David Talbort in *Contemporary Ethiopia,* it "is probable that not much more than half of ... [the landowners in Shoa Province pay] tax direct to the government owing to the large amount of exemption through the *rist-gult"* and other exceptions.

Siso-gult—⅔ of the land possessed by the first settlers was taken by the government. The ⅓ remaining was his *siso* [tax-free portion of land]. In some cases the settler was allowed to retain only ¼ of his previous holding. The remaining ¾ was taken by the government. The government allowed the settler to retain his ⅓ or ¼ and imposed just a nominal tax on it pending its development. The system and rate of land taxation on *siso* land is the same as for *rist-gult.* The basic difference between *rist-gult* and *siso-gult* lies in their origin, the former being a government grant for services rendered, and the latter the result of government expropriation of land with tax-free privileges for the remainder as payment.

Samon—The *samon* exemption in the 1944 Proclamation applies to lands held by the Ethiopian Orthodox Church. There are 2 major land tenure systems relating to the Church: *samon* and Church *gult. Samon* refers to land in which the "primary interest" has been vested in the Church. This interest carried the right to collect, and retain for Church use, land tax and tithe

from persons settled on the land. This right was institutionalized in Decree No. 2 of Mar. 10, 1942. All taxes mentioned above are, according to this decree, collected by the
Church and deposited in the Church treasury. The collected
money is to be used for the maintenance of the Church. Church
gult is landed property granted by the government to the
Church, which the Church in turn apportions among its
ecclesiastical members. Each holder must pay to the Church a
tithe which is established by the Church, until he terminates his
period of service. The person who then succeeds him takes over
the land and follows the same practice. Holders of Church *gult*
can in turn rent or parcel out land and demand taxes and rent
from tenants.

Thus, by Decree No. 2 of 1942 and the additional exemption granted in the Land Tax Proclamation of 1944, the Church
pays no taxes at all to the government of Ethiopia. In fact,
because of these laws, the Church has become a government
within the government of Ethiopia. Though yearly figures as to
what the Church receives in taxes are almost impossible to
obtain, it is known that in the 1961-2 fiscal year, the total land
taxes paid to the Church were E\$1,981,148. This was 11½% of
the total revenue from the same sources for the whole country.
Command of this revenue makes the Church an economic
power as well as a political, social and cultural one.

It was proclaimed in 1942 that every landowner would be
liable to pay the land tax. But this liability was no longer in
effect in 1944. Christopher Clapham commented in *The Institutions of the Central Ethiopian Government:* "If the emperor
influences ... groups, they also influence him, for he can only
keep them under his authority if he can maintain some
consensus by granting some of the aims of each."

The movement by the government during 1942-4 from a
universal to a more particularistic outlook *vis a vis* the formulation and application of the land tax laws indicated to some
observers that the government had become more realistic about
Ethiopia's traditional forces. The landed elite and the Ethiopian
Orthodox Church were resistant to any government attempts
to delimit their power bases. Both these groups directly or
indirectly made it clear to Haile Selassie that they would not
accept his centralized land tax of 1942. They forced the
emperor to retreat, according to some analysts, and as a result

the 1942 land tax proclamation was voided by the issuance of the 1944 proclamation, which was full of exemptions.

Income Tax

In an additional move aimed at modernizing and improving government fiscal practices, Haile Selassie May 29, 1944 issued a Personal & Business Tax Proclamation— Proclamation No. 60 of 1944. Its provisions were retroactive to Sept. 12, 1943. The taxes were levied equally on all income levels despite wide agreement among many fiscal authorities that, at least in the early stages of capitalistic development, it was preferable to tax the rich more heavily than the poor. It appeared that the emperor found opposition among the landed elite; as a result, a progressive income tax was not introduced in terms of yearly earnings.

The income tax was divided into 3 separate schedules. Schedule "A" imposed a tax amounting to approximately 5% of the taxpayer's yearly earnings. Schedule "B" levied a fixed tax, irrespective of income, on brokers, importers and exporters, oil companies, flour mills, breweries, retailers, hotels, restaurants, bars, garages and tanneries. Schedule "C" imposed a special surtax on all persons and businesses with yearly income in excess of US$25,000.

The Finance Ministry was made responsible for the collection of income taxes. An appeals committee was established to handle grievances; the committee was made up of 16 members, all chosen by Haile Selassie. (E$2½ million was collected in income taxes in the fiscal year 1944-5.)

The Personal & Business Tax Proclamation of 1944 was amended Aug. 27, 1949 in a move to attract more foreign investments. The 1949 Proclamation provided that "every business presenting the character of a long-term investment in an industrial, transport or mining enterprise, and sustaining an investment in the first year of not less than E$200,000, shall, in the first year of operation and for the period in which such investment continues but not to exceed 5 years from the date of the establishment of the business, be granted an exemption of income tax."

A commission composed of 6 members, 3 chosen by the Finance Ministry and 3 by the merchants of the "empire," was created to advise the finance minister on classifying taxpayers. The tax appeal committee was reduced in number to 7 members chosen by the emperor. Schedule "A" was altered by exempting from income tax liability people earning less than E$300. The annual levy under Schedule "A" ranged from E$5 for incomes between E$300 and E$500 to a tax of E$15,000 on incomes between E$90,000 and E$100,000. The tax was E$20 on E$1,000-to-E$1,500 incomes, E$60 on E$2,000-to-E$2,500 incomes, E$240 on E$5,000-to-E$5,500 incomes, E$600 on E$10,000-to-E$11,000 incomes, E$3,600 on E$25,000-to-E$30,000 incomes and E$9,000 on E$50,000-to-E$60,000 incomes.

Schedule "B" excluded importers and exporters from the fixed tax but added a number of different firms to the 1944 tax list. Schedule "C" required exporters and importers to pay a tax based on the value of their merchandise. In addition a special 10% surtax was added whenever the profits of a business exceeded E$100,000.

Other Taxes

A customs office was set up in 1943, and export duties of 10% to 30% were announced.

Proclamation No. 94 of 1947 established an education tax amounting to 30% of the sum of the land tax and tithe payable on land. The tax was collected by the Finance Ministry for the central government, but the money was redistributed later to the provincial governments. Depending upon the needs of the provinces, in some years not all the collected money was returned, while in other years more was returned than was collected.

Court System & Police

A systematised judiciary was established Jan. 31, 1942 under a Justice Proclamation. The court system consisted of a Supreme Imperial Court, a High Court, provincial courts and regional and communal courts.

The Supreme Imperial Court is staffed by 3 judges, 2 nominated from among judges sitting in the High Court and one chosen by the emperor.

The High Court consists of as many judges as the emperor sees fit to appoint. The High Court is deemed to be fully constituted for a hearing when 3 judges are present.

The provincial courts sit in each province and comprise as many judges as the emperor decides to appoint. 3 members constitute a quorum. The jurisdiction of a provincial court is limited in criminal matters to "imprisonment not exceeding 5 years; corporal punishment not exceeding 5 lashes."

Regional and communal courts, inferior to provincial courts, may be established as or if the emperor sees fit.

All courts have jurisdiction in criminal and civil cases.

The Supreme Imperial Court, theoretically, has final jurisdiction over appeals. Traditionally, however, the emperor is the highest court of appeal; this tradition has been maintained despite the establishment of the court system.

A police force, established by Proclamation No. 6 of 1942, came into effect Jan. 31, 1942. As provided by the proclamation, "the force shall consist of such number of superior police officers, inspectors, non-commissioned officers and constables as our minister of interior may from time to time direct." A police commissioner, appointed by the interior minister, heads the force.

Arrest warrants are usually unnecessary when an individual is apprehended, but, with few exceptions, searches on private property may not be made without warrants.

The Council of Ministers (Cabinet)

Although the emperor's cabinet was institutionalized under the 1931 Constitution, Order* No. 1 of Jan. 29, 1943 defined the powers of the various ministers and established the office of the prime minister. In addition, Order No. 1 formally set up the Council of Ministers (cabinet).

Order No. 1 specified that the Council of Ministers is made up of all ministers and vice ministers under the chairmanship of the emperor. In the emperor's absence, a minister nominated by him chairs cabinet meetings. The Council of Ministers acts in

---

* Orders are issued by the emperor when parliament is not in session, and they are presented to parliament for its approval when it convenes.

an advisory capacity to the emperor, and ministers are held jointly responsible for decisions taken in any council meeting. Before anybody can accept a post as a cabinet member, he must swear allegiance to both government and emperor. In addition to advising the emperor, ministers may draft laws applying to their ministries, and these drafts are discussed at council meetings.

Order No. 1 created 11 ministries: Communications & Public Works, Education & Fine Arts, Commerce & Industry, Interior, Agriculture, Foreign Affairs, Finance, War, Justice, and Posts, Telephones & Telegraph. The Ministry of the Pen is the keeper of the seal; it sends out all the emperor's orders. Christopher Clapham asserted in *Haile Selassie's Government* that in 1943 Minister of the Pen Walda-Giyorgis Walda-Yohanes, because of his ability to influence Haile Selassie, "was [with the exception of the emperor] the outstanding figure of the time and probably the most powerful politician in Ethiopia."

Major Officials

In order to ensure his personal control and to keep the political and administrative elite weak and off-guard, Emperor Haile Selassie constantly shifts his personnel. These are among the most important officials appointed by the emperor after his return to Ethiopia:

Mulughetta Buli—appointed commander of the Emperor's Guard May 10, 1941 and promoted from major to brigadier general July 3, 1949.

Makonnen Endalkachio—appointed interior minister May 10, 1941.

Blatengueta Lorenzo Taezaz—appointed foreign affairs minister May 10, 1941.

Makonnen Desta—appointed education minister May 10, 1941; shifted to Posts, Telephones & Telegraphs Ministry May 29, 1944; appointed governor general of Wollega Province July 3, 1949.

Araye Abebe—appointed posts, telephones and telegraph minister July 3, 1949.

Ras Abebe Aregai—appointed war minister Feb. 10, 1942; appointed interior minister July 3, 1949.

Makonnen Habte Wold—appointed agriculture minister Feb. 21, 1942; shifted to Commerce & Industry Ministry 2 years later; appointed finance minister July 3, 1949.

Ephrem Twelde Medhin—appointed agriculture minister July 3, 1949.

Yilma Deressa—vice minister of finance in 1942; became acting education minister in 1945 and commerce and industry minister July 3, 1949.

Tschafe Taezaz Wold Wuiorguis—appointed justice minister July 3, 1949.

Aklilou Habte Wold—appointed foreign affairs minister July 3, 1949.

Ras Imru—appointed governor general of Beghemder Province May 17, 1944.

Zaude Belayneth—appointed health minister July 3, 1949.

Local Government

One of Haile Selassie's major programs was to institutionalize local government yet put it under the authority of the central government in Addis Ababa. Decree* No. 1 of Aug. 27, 1942 set up a new adminstrative structure for local government, and this decree is still the basis on which local administration is conducted.

In the case of the local-government decree, the emperor used centralization to overcome the traditional forces that had helped him to the throne but that then sought to limit his freedom of action. His method was to promote modernization by centralizing the authority of the government and then creating a multiplicity of political institutions to carry out the government's demands.

Decree No. 1 of 1942 set up the political subdivisions of the empire and established corresponding political roles. Each province was placed under the responsibility of one governor general, who is appointed by the emperor on the recommendation of the interior minister. Each governor general is responsible to a cabinet minister, according to the activity he may be involved in. The governor general supervises the collection of

* A Decree is a law promulgated directly by the emperor without the necessity of parliamentary approval. It is the same as a proclamation.

taxes and must see to it that government regulations are
carried out in his province.

The governor general is assisted by a director appointed by
the emperor. The decree provides that "the director shall supervise, under the governor general, the expenditure of the funds
legally provided for the province" by the central government.
The maintenance of archives and the coordination of secretarial work is directed by a principal secretariat, also selected
by the emperor. In addition, a provincial council was instituted
to "advise on matters relating to the welfare of the inhabitants
and the prosperity of the province." This council consists of the
governor general as chairman, the principal secretary, the
director, the chief police officer of the area concerned and the
governors of the subprovinces within the province.

Although this is a decentralized structure, it is not lawfully
an autonomous structure. According to the decree: "As the emperor grants and withdraws titles, appointments and honors,
the governor general or officials under him cannot directly
appoint or dismiss or relieve from duty, or transfer anyone."

Each province is subdivided into subprovinces (*awurajas*),
which are themselves divided into districts (*waredas*), which are
further divided into subdistricts (*mektil-waredas*). (There are 14
provinces, 103 subprovinces, 505 districts and 1,949 subdistricts.) Each subprovince has a governor, appointed by the
emperor, whose duty it is to administer the *awuraja*. He is
directly responsible to the governor general. A council advises
the governor and is made up of the governor, his principal
secretary and officials of ministries who are stationed in the
subprovince. A similar structure exists in the districts and
subdistricts.

The local government system is a vertical political structure with a system of checks and balances that exist both within
and outside of each political division. Margery Perham asserted
in *The Government of Ethiopia* that to check both traditional
and modern influences, "the emperor found it necessary to
appoint older men of standing" as governors while "to give
scope and practical expression to the desire for reforms of the
younger men who had received some education, the emperor
appointed some of these as directors." This type of placement is
common in Ethiopia, where the middle level of government
administration is staffed largely by members of the educated

elite and the upper level by persons drawn from traditional groups.

Decree No. 1 states that the emperor "shall determine the military forces necessary" for the security of a province. Each province is to have a military commander appointed by the emperor, and only this commander may issue orders to the military forces. "In the event of serious disturbance in the province beyond the powers of the police to cope with, the governor general is authorized to call upon the military forces in his province for assistance. When circumstances permit, he must first of all consult with a commission consisting of the senior officials of the various ministries who may be present, the commanding officer and 5 chief elders, and must also notify the superior authority of his intention to call upon the military forces for assistance and shall await his instructions."

PERIOD OF GROWTH: 1950-4

The years 1950-4 witnessed an impressive expansion of economic, educational and other domestic programs in Ethiopia, but during this period there was also evident a marked concentration by Ethiopia on international affairs: A rapprochement with Italy took place; Ethiopia sent troops to fight under the UN flag in Korea; Eritrea federated with Ethiopia under a UN plan, and the UN also settled the issue of Somaliland; the U.S. granted aid to Ethiopia for internal development, and a military assistance pact was signed by Ethiopia and the U.S.

Education

With a literacy rate estimated at 5%, Ethiopia initially emphasized elementary and secondary schools. In his program for modernizing the country, however, the emperor needed skilled and educated administrators, and he therefore pressed ahead with plans for institutions of higher education.

The University College of Addis Ababa was opened Feb. 27, 1951. Haile Selassie said at the inaugural ceremonies: "We are proud to see Ethiopian youth thirsting for learning. Although the fruits of education can be applied to evil as well as to good things, you Ethiopian students should avoid having a bad reputation and be eager and energetic in your studies, be loyal to your country and obedient to your teachers, eschew lies and follow truth, respect good and be heirs of good work."

The College of Agriculture in Harar Province was also opened in 1951 and the College of Engineering in Addis Ababa in 1953.

(The Haile Selassie I Military Academy was officially opened by the emperor in Harar Oct. 6, 1958. The academy was charged with the task of training officers of the Ethiopian army and of the Imperial Body Guard. The first commander of the academy was Col. N. C. Rawlley, a member of the Indian army, as were 9 other officers on the staff.)

Land Taxes Revised

Responding to pressure from landowners, the emperor in 1951 agreed to modifications of the Land Tax Proclamation of 1944. In Proclamation No. 117 of 1951, issued June 28, the government divided unmeasured land into these 5 categories, with each category of unmeasured land assessed at its own rate of tax and tithe:

Categories	1	2	3	4	5
Land tax (per *gasha*)	E$8	E$7	E$6	E$4	E$2
Tithe (per *gasha*)	E$12	E$10	E$9	E$6	E$3

The basis of differentiation among the 5 categories was not discussed. The implication was that there existed a difference in fertility of soil, and since distinct categories had been established previously for measured lands, the same would be done for unmeasured lands. The government maintained that 5 categories were necessary. This was based on the premise that unmeasured lands are generally of lower fertility than measured lands, and, therefore, a wider range of delineation was necessary. This was also considered a case of regressive taxation meant to pacify owners of large land holdings, who clearly owned more unmeasured than measured land and could place this land in the lower tax brackets. The fact that no basis exists on which to separate the 5 categories of land lends support to this argument. Eshetu Chole asserted (in "Taxation and Economic Development in Ethiopia"—*Ethiopia Observer,* Vol. II, No. 1, 1967) that "people of wealth and higher position [in Ethiopia] pay lower taxes or are exempted wholly, and on the contrary, the poorer the man and the more humble his position, the heavier is the burden of taxation."

Legal Notice* No. 154 of 1951 was issued June 28 to complement Proclamation No. 117. The notice established, for the first time, a decentralized structure with powers to classify unmeasured *gabbar* land. It also established an appeal commission empowered to adjudicate disputes that might occur between land assessors and landowners. In terms of land taxation, this was an unprecedented move on the part of the govern-

---

*Legal Notices are subsidiary legislation signed by a minister under a proclamation that usually gives the minister concerned power to legislate thereunder.

ment, which recognized that the Finance Ministry in Addis Ababa could pursue the goals of the tax laws only by shifting a limited amount of power into the provinces. It was meant to apply only to unmeasured *gabbar* lands.

Under the 1951 Legal Notice, the classification of unmeasured *gabbar* land was to be made by an assessment committee consisting of: one representative each from the Interior Ministry and Finance Ministry, sent from Addis Ababa; the governor and *chiqa shum* (tribal chief) of the district concerned; the governor of the subdistrict concerned, and 2 elders selected by inhabitants of the subdistrict. The member from the Interior Ministry was to serve as chairman. The Finance Ministry was given the power to assign to each district a clerk for writing out the assessment and to handle secretarial work relating to appeals.

An appeal commission was established; it consisted of the governor of the province (as chairman), the treasurer of the province, the *chiqa shum* of the area concerned and 2 elders selected by the inhabitants of the subdistrict involved.

No standards were established to classify land. All that the members of the assessment committees were aware of was that there were 5 categories of unmeasured land differentiated only by soil fertility. With no concrete guidelines, the assessment committees could operate relatively independent from Addis Ababa. In fact, since no universal norms existed, the basis of measurement could differ from subdistrict to subdistrict. The only functional checks placed on the assessment committees were the appeal commission, local conditions, which might differ from district to district, and the Interior Ministry representative, who, as chairman and spokesman for the loose norms of Addis Ababa, could, at times, influence the committee.

The appeal commission could act on claims by both landowner and the Finance Ministry, if either believed that the assessment committee had erred. Decisions of the appeal commission were by majority vote and were to be implemented by the governor of the subdistrict.

Local conditions served to check the power of the assessment committee. In Gojam, for instance, where communal land tenure exists, the citizenry would not permit assessment teams on their land. To avoid a repetition of the crisis of 1942, the government did not contest the barring of the assessment teams. (Clashes between Ethiopian troops and armed peasant tax rebels in Gojam had been reported Aug. 2, 1950.)

Other Taxes

A cattle tax was instituted under a proclamation issued Sept. 30, 1954. Each owner of cattle, goats, sheep, pigs, camels, horses and mules was required to pay a specific amount per animal—E$1 per pig, 50 Ethiopian cents per camel, 25¢ per head of cattle, horse and mule and 5¢ per goat and sheep.

According to rules established under the Cattle Tax Proclamation, it was up to the animal breeder to bring his animals to an appointed spot for the animals to be counted. Animal breeders thus could keep some of their animals from the counting spot. In addition, many people who live on Ethiopia's Somalian border drive their cattle across the border when the time comes for the cattle to be counted for tax purposes. It is almost impossible for the Ethiopian government to prevent this.

(It is estimated that there are 65 million taxable animals in Ethiopia.)

As a further incentive for investment in Ethiopia, the Personal & Business Tax Proclamation of Aug. 27, 1949 was amended Nov. 30, 1954 by this addition: "Income derived from rent of new buildings shall, from the date of their completion and from the start of rent collection therefrom, be free from tax for a period of 3 years."

'Republican Plot' Crushed

Recurrent opposition to the imperial regime was brought to the surface again in 1951 with the announcement that a new "plot" had been crushed. A special tribunal in Addis Ababa sentenced 8 men, including Bitwoded Negash, ex-president of parliament, to death July 26 for plotting to assassinate Haile Selassie and set up an Ethiopian republic.

Eritrea Federates with Ethiopia

On the occasion of the opening of the 4th UN General Assembly session in New York Sept. 20, 1949, Haile Selassie had proposed that the UN turn over the former Italian colonies of Eritrea and Somaliland to Ethiopia. The 2 territories at that time were still occupied by Britain, and the UN had started considering their future in 1947. In 1950 the UN agreed to the union of Eritrea, but not Somaliland, with Ethiopia. (At the time of the Ethiopian-Eritrean federation, Eritrea had a population of about a million people, most of them Muslims.)

The federation of Eritrea with Ethiopia was approved by the UN General Assembly by 46-10 vote Dec. 2, 1950. Ethiopia had sought to annex Eritrea but accepted a federation as a compromise. Italy had wanted to keep Eritrea but agreed to the UN decision. The UN resolution provided that the union was to be achieved by Sept. 15, 1952. Eritrea was to have home rule, but its foreign policy was to be controlled by Ethiopia, and a customs union set-up was to give Ethiopia free access to the Red Sea. The resolution also called for a federal legislature with representation based on population. The people of the 2 states were to become a single nationality as subjects of the emperor.

Dr. Eduardo Anze Matienzo of Bolivia, UN commissioner for Eritrea, announced Oct. 7, 1951 that Eritrea had accepted the UN federation plan.

Elections to a temporary Representative Assembly, whose function was to approve a draft constitution for Eritrea, were held in Eritrea Mar. 25 and 26, 1952, and 68 members evenly divided between Muslims and Coptic Christians were chosen.

The new assembly convened in Asmara Apr. 28, and Anze Matienzo May 3 submitted a draft constitution to establish Eritrea as an autonomous unit federated with Ethiopia under the sovereignty of the Ethiopian crown. Anze Matienzo had prepared the draft after consulting with prominent Eritreans and with international experts on constitutional law. The draft was unanimously adopted by the assembly July 10 and was ratified Aug. 11 by Haile Selassie.

The new constitution provided that Eritrea should have legislative, executive and judicial powers in matters not reserved to the federal government. (These non-federal powers included authority over law and internal police, health, education, public assistance and social security, protection of labor, exploitation of national resources, the regulation of industry and trade, agriculture, domestic communications, public utilities, the Eritrean budget and taxes to meet the expenses of Eritrea.) Eritrea was to bear its share of expenses for federal functions and services and was to levy federal taxes by delegation from the federal government.

The constitution further provided that a representative of the Ethiopian emperor in Eritrea would maintain permanent contact between the 2 governments and would handle conflicts of jurisdiction.

Under the new constitution, full executive power was given to a chief executive, who would be elected by the Eritrean Assembly but would not be politically responsible to it. Secretaries of departments would be appointed by him and would be responsible only to him. (Tedla Bairu was elected chief executive of Eritrea Aug. 28, 1952.)

The unicameral Eritrean Assembly would be elected by all adult males of federal nationality who had been resident in their Eritrean constituency for at least a year. Judges would be appointed by the chief executive on the recommendation of the president of the assembly, who would recommend 2 candidates for each appointment from a list supplied by a committee composed of the president of the Supreme Court and 2 judges. The constitution provided for the protection of the accepted human rights in general plus the special rights of various groups; it guaranteed respect for their customs, traditions, religious beliefs and way of life, their personal status, their property rights and their right to use their own language.

Emperor Haile Selassie signed the Eritrean-Ethiopian federation act Sept. 11, 1952, and Eritrea became an independent (federated) nation Sept. 15. The last British occupation troops left Eritrea Sept. 16 and were replaced by Ethiopian troops. Prince Andargue Kassai, a son-in-law of Haile Selassie, was chosen by the emperor Sept. 13 to be his representative in Eritrea.

The official unification of Eritrea and Ethiopia was effected in Asmara, Eritrea Oct. 4. Haile Selassie entered Asmara and was welcomed enthusiastically by large crowds.

(Haile Selassie said May 26, 1954 that the U.S. had played an important role in helping to unify Eritrea and Ethiopia.)

(As for Italian Somaliland, the UN Trusteeship Council Jan. 27, 1950 approved an agreement with Italy restoring the colony to Italy as a UN trust territory for 10 years, after which Somaliland was to become independent. The UN General Assembly approved the agreement Dec. 2, 1950 by 44-6 vote. Somalia gained its independence June 26, 1960.)

Ethiopian Troops Fight in Korea

North Korean troops invaded South Korea June 25, 1950. The UN Security Council the same day passed a resolution calling for the immediate cessation of hostilities, requesting that North Korea withdraw its armed forces from South Korea and asking "all [UN] members to render every assistance to the United Nations in the execution of this resolution." The Security Council June 27 passed a further resolution that called for "urgent military measures ... as may be necessary to repel the armed attack and to restore international peace and security in the area."

Ethiopia responded to the UN appeal for troops to be sent to South Korea, under UN command, to fight against North Korean forces there. After 6 months of training, an expeditionary force of 1,158 Ethiopian officers and men, under the command of Col. Kebede Gebre, left Ethiopia Apr. 16, 1951 and arrived in Korea May 6.

Haile Selassie Apr. 14 had told the Ethiopian force, known as the Kagnew Battalion: "You have been called upon to represent amongst the armed forces of many friendly nations, engaged in the same high endeavor, the heritage of a people that, for untold centuries, has fiercely fought to defend its freedom and independence. In the dark hours [of the Italian invasion of Ethiopia] when we and our people were called upon to fight, we did not fail, and today, thanks to that determination, Ethiopia has again resumed her rightful place amongst the United Nations. Of all the nations of the world, the name of Ethiopia has been most closely associated with the principle [of collective security]. Our undaunted defense of collective security at the League of Nations, our own appeal to that august body, our fierce and unaided struggles throughout [the Italian invasion], have given to Ethiopia an imperishable place in the history of that principle in modern times. That is why, as sovereign head of Ethiopia and as commander-in-chief of the Ethiopian armed forces, we did not hesitate immediately to respond to the appeal for collective assistance launched by the United Nations following the aggression in Korea."

(Ethiopian replacements and reinforcements were sent to Korea later. At least 80 Ethiopian soldiers were reported killed in Korea before the fighting was ended by an armistice July 27, 1953.)

Foreign Relations & Foreign Aid

More than 10 years after the ouster of the Italian invaders of his country, Haile Selassie Sept. 7, 1951 accepted the credentials of an ambassador from the post-Fascist Italian republic. Receiving Italian envoy Alfonso Tacoli, the emperor said: "We welcome you to our court as a representative of a people who, we would believe, would resolutely reject all past and future policies of aggression.... Our final and friendly reconciliation should be a sign of encouragement and a contribution to the strengthening of world peace."

Full diplomatic relations between Ethiopia and Yugoslavia were established Mar. 4, 1952.

Ethiopia received a US$1.4 million loan from the International Bank for Reconstruction & Development (World Bank) Feb. 19, 1951 to expand its phone and telegraph system.

Ethiopia signed a Point 4 technical aid agreement with the U.S. May 15, 1952.

Ethiopia and the U.S. May 22, 1953 signed a mutual defense agreement under which the U.S. promised to supply military advisers to help train Ethiopian armed forces. Under the treaty, Ethiopia May 14, 1954 granted the U.S. the right to build and maintain military bases in Ethiopia for 99 years. The U.S. in 1954 opened a global communications base, Kagnew Station, in Asmara, Eritrea.

A treaty of friendship and commerce between the U.S. and Ethiopia was ratified by the U.S. Senate July 21, 1953, and the ratified instrument was signed by Pres. Dwight D. Eisenhower Aug. 6.

In his first trip abroad as emperor, Haile Selassie left Ethiopia for the U.S. May 19, 1954. Addressing a joint session of the U.S. Congress May 26, the emperor thanked Americans for their "valuable support," given "through mutual security and technical assistance agreements." He called their attention to "Ethiopia as a factor in world politics." Ethiopia's "geographic location is of great significance," he said. "Ethiopia occupies a unique position on the most constricted but important of strategic lines of communications in the world, that which passes through the Red Sea. She also lies on the other most strategic line of communications in the world, namely the world band of telecommunications."

(The U.S. Foreign Operations Administration reported May 27, 1955 that during the period Apr. 3, 1948 to Mar. 31, 1955, the U.S. had allotted $8,612,000 in foreign aid to Ethiopia.)

After leaving the U.S., Haile Selassie visited Canada, Mexico, Yugoslavia, Greece, Britain, France, the Netherlands, West Germany, Sweden, Norway, Denmark, Switzerland and Austria in the first such tour undertaken by an Ethiopian monarch. He arrived back in Ethiopia Dec. 6, 1954. (Pres. Tito of Yugoslavia, repaying the emperor's visit, spent 2 weeks in Ethiopia in Dec. 1955.)

REVISED CONSTITUTION: 1955

1955 was a key year for Haile Selassie's policy of modernization and institutionalization. The emperor made major changes in cabinet and other posts, and he promulgated a revised constitution that extended the roles of various political institutions, created new ones and carried further the effort to decentralize the central government. Although the Ethiopian government remained in 1955 a mixed traditional and modern regime, it appeared that the constitution was written, at least in part, to increase the strength of the modernizing elements.

Personnel Changes

Walda-Giyorgis Walda-Yohanes, minister of the pen and the most powerful member of Emperor Haile Selassie's cabinet, was removed from his position Apr. 28, 1955 and appointed governor general of Arussi Province in southern Ethiopia. In effect, the emperor demoted him and stripped him of his great power. Walda-Yohanes was succeeded as minister of the pen by Tsahafe Tezaz Tafarra Worq, the emperor's private secretary. Makonnen Desta, governor general of Wollega Province since July 7, 1949, was appointed Apr. 28 to the new post of minister of culture.

The emperor June 4, 1955 made these additional shifts in high-level posts: Interior Min. Ras Abebe Aregai was appointed defense minister. Mesfin Sileshi, lord chamberlain to the imperial palace, was appointed interior minister. Akale-Worq Habte Wold was appointed to the new post of vice minister for social affairs. Brig. Gen. Mulughetta Buli, commander of the emperor's bodyguard, was appointed chief of staff of the army with the rank of major general.

The 1955 Constitution

A new constitution was promulgated by Haile Selassie Nov. 4, 1955 in the midst of the 3-day (Nov. 3-5) celebration of the 25th anniversary of his accession to the throne. The revised charter, superseding the Constitution of 1931, was presented at a special session of the Ethiopian Senate and Chamber of Deputies in a ceremony attended by foreign guests and Ethiopian leaders from all parts of the nation. The emperor said that one of the reasons for revising the constitution was the need for the structure of government to "grow in size and in power."

The 1955 Constitution established new institutions in the executive office and increased the power of parliament.

As revised, the executive office included the Council of Ministers (cabinet), the Crown Council and the emperor.

The Council of Ministers, consisting of a prime minister and all the cabinet ministers, is an advisory body that meets regularly. The prime minister is the spokesman of the emperor in parliament. He and the cabinet ministers serve with no fixed term of office and are appointed by the emperor. This body was institutionalized in Article 69 of the 1955 Constitution. All draft bills and issues of importance go to the Council of Ministers for study. The council then presents its recommendations to the emperor. The draft bill, along with the recommendation of the council, is then presented to the Crown Council.

The Crown Council consists of the archbishop of the Ethiopian Orthodox Church, the president of the Senate and other dignitaries appointed by the emperor. According to Christopher Clapham, in his unpublished Ph.D. thesis *The Institutions of the Central Ethiopian Government:* "It may be ... inferred that one of the main features of the [Crown] Council [is] to represent the traditional elite...." The Crown Council, institutionalized under Article 70 of the 1955 Constitution, is presided over by the emperor or a member designated by him. "Decisions made in council and approved by the emperor shall be communicated by the prime minister to parliament in the form of proposals for legislation."

The 1955 Constitution expanded the powers of parliament by requiring that proposed legislation be submitted to parliament and that, in order to become law, such legislation receive the approval of both the Senate and the Chamber of Deputies. Senators continued to be appointed by the emperor from among princes and other dignitaries, but members of the Chamber of Deputies were to be elected by universal suffrage.

Article 26 of the 1955 Constitution affirms, however, that "the sovereignty of the empire is vested in the emperor, and the supreme authority over all the affairs of the empire is exercised by him as the head of state." The emperor, thus, remains with no formal restraint on his power. Article 4 says: "The person of the emperor is sacred. His dignity is inviolable and his power indisputable."

Abridged text of the revised Constitution of 1955:

CONQUERING LION OF THE TRIBE OF JUDAH
HAILE SELASSIE I
ELECT OF GOD, EMPEROR OF ETHIOPIA

Whereas, 24 years ago, at the beginning of our reign, we granted to our faithful subjects and proclaimed a constitution for the empire of Ethiopia; and...

Whereas, being desirous of consolidating the progress achieved and of laying a solid basis for the happiness and prosperity of the present and future generations of our people, we have prepared a revised constitution for our empire...; and

Whereas, our parliament, after due examination and deliberation, has submitted to us its approval of this revised constitution;

Now therefore, we Haile Selassie I, emperor of Ethiopia, do, on the occasion of the 25th anniversary of our coronation, hereby proclaim and place into force and effect as from today, the revised constitution of the empire of Ethiopia....

Given in our imperial capital, on this the 4th day of November 1955 and on the 25th anniversary of our coronation.

Haile Selassie I
Emperor

Tsahafe Tezaz Tafarra Worq
Minister of the Pen

CHAPTER I—THE ETHIOPIAN EMPIRE & THE SUCCESSION TO THE THRONE

Article 1. The empire of Ethiopia comprises all the territories, including the islands and the territorial waters, under the sovereignty of the Ethiopian crown. Its sovereignty and territory are indivisible. Its territories and the sovereign rights therein are inalienable.

All Ethiopian subjects, whether living within or without the empire, constitute the Ethiopian people.

Article 2. The imperial dignity shall remain perpetually attached to the line of Haile Selassie I, descendant of King Sahle Selassie, whose line descends without interruption from the dynasty of Menelik I, son of the Queen of Ethiopia, the Queen of Sheba, and King Solomon of Jerusalem.

Article 3. The succession to the throne and crown of the empire by the descendants of the emperor and the exercise of the powers of regency shall be determined as hereinafter provided.

Article 4. By virtue of his imperial blood, as well as by the anointing which he has received, the person of the emperor is sacred. His dignity is inviolable and his power indisputable. He is, consequently, entitled to all the honors due to him in accordance with tradition and the present constitution. Anyone so bold as to seek to injure the emperor will be punished.

Article 5. The order of succession shall be lineal, and only male, born in lawful wedlock, may succeed male; the nearest line shall pass before the more remote, and the elder in line before the younger....

Article 6. Among those entitled to the succession shall be reckoned also the son unborn, who shall immediately take his proper place in the line of succession the moment he is born into the world.

Article 7. In the event that, at the time of his succession to the throne and crown, the emperor shall have attained the age of 18 years, he shall, on the day determined by him, but in any event not later than one year after his succession to the crown, be anointed and crowned as emperor....

Article 8. Regency shall exist in the event that the emperor is unable to exercise the imperial office, whether by reason of minority, absence from the empire, or by reason of serious illness as determined by the Crown Council. In such cases, the regency shall exercise, in the name of the emperor, all the powers and prerogatives of the crown, except that the regency shall have no power to grant the title of prince, and shall have caretaker powers only as regards the properties of the crown and of the emperor. Regency shall automatically terminate upon the cessation, as regards the emperor, of the conditions having given rise to the regency....

Article 9. In the event that the emperor, or in the event that the crown prince or the heir presumptive, in the situations provided for in Article 11, shall not have attained the age of 18 years, the regency shall be exercised by the Council of Regency as provided for in Article 11.

Article 10. The Council of Regency shall consist of the empress mother, the 2 descendants of the line of Sahle Selassie most nearly related to the emperor, as determined by the Crown Council, having reached the age of 18 and being of sound mind, the archbishop, the prime minister, the president of the Senate and the president of the Chamber of Deputies. The president of the Council of Regency shall be the empress mother, or, in her absence, the prime minister. No decisions of the Council of Regency shall be taken except by a majority vote of $\frac{2}{3}$ of the members thereof.

Article 11. Regency shall be exercised by the crown prince or the heir presumptive, as the case may be, in case of the serious illness, or the absence of the emperor from the empire. However, in the event that the crown prince or the heir presumptive, as the case may be, himself shall be subject to serious illness, or shall be absent from the empire or shall not have attained his 18th year, the regency shall be exercised by the Council of Regency, which shall automatically relinquish its functions to the crown prince or the heir presumptive, as the case may be, upon the cessation of any such disability of the crown prince or the heir presumptive, as the case may be. . . .

Article 12. Upon the birth of the crown prince, the emperor shall designate the members of the Council of Guardianship to be convened and to assume its responsibilities only in the event of a regency. The mother of the crown prince shall be *ex-officio* a member of such council. The Council of Guardianship shall receive in trust for the crown prince ⅓ of the annual income and revenues received by the predecessor of the crown prince who has become emperor, in conformity with the provisions of Article 19 (c).

Article 13. (a) In the event that the emperor shall, at any time, have no male descendant, or no male descendant capable of meeting the requirements for succession to the throne, he shall, after having previously consulted the Crown Council, publicly designate as heir presumptive from amongst his nearest male relatives, a direct descendant of Sahle Selassie, meeting the requirements for succession to the throne. (b) The determinations as to the qualifications for succession shall be made by the emperor, after having previously consulted the Crown Council. (c) In case of a determination that a male descendant is incapable of meeting the requirements for succession, such determination shall operate to exclude such male descendant in favor of the next male descendant or in favor of the heir presumptive. The designation of an heir presumptive shall become inoperative upon the subsequent birth of a male descendant. (d) In case of the minority of the emperor, the designation of an heir presumptive shall ... be effected by the Council of Regency. However, at the time of his coronation, and at any time thereafter, the emperor shall be free to designate ... another heir presumptive in replacement of the heir presumptive designated. . . .

Article 14. Throughout his minority, the place of residence of the emperor shall be the imperial palace. Absence therefrom for travel or for educational purposes may be authorized by law. Upon attaining the age of 12 years, the emperor may make official appearances, attended by the Council of Regency, the princes ... and the dignitaries *(mekuanent).*

Article 15. Any member of the imperial family, who, being eligible for the succession, marries a foreigner or who marries without the consent of the emperor, of the regent or of the Council of Regency, as the case may be, shall forfeit all imperial prerogatives for himself and his descendants.

Article 16. The imperial family shall include all direct lineal ascendants and descendants, together with their spouses, of the emperor, with the exception of those who have not complied with the provisions of Article 15 or who are not of the Ethiopian Orthodox faith.

Article 17. The status, position, duties, responsibilities, privileges, emoluments, travels abroad and deportment of the princes and of members of the imperial family shall be considered by the Crown Council from time to time and their recommendations thereon shall be communicated to the emperor for further action.

In the event that the aforesaid oath shall not have been taken on the occasion of the coronation, either by the crown prince or by the heir presumptive, as the case may be, it shall be taken before the emperor by the crown prince or the heir presumptive, as the case may be, upon his attaining the age of 18.

Article 18. Upon the death of the emperor, there shall be a period of full national mourning of 3 months, followed by a period of half mourning of 6 months, and upon the death of the empress, there shall be a period of full national mourning of 2 months, followed by a period of half mourning of 4 months. The emperor shall proclaim lesser periods of full and half national mournings upon the deaths of other members of the imperial family, except that no period of national mourning may cause to be postponed a coronation more than one year from the date of the succession to the crown of the emperor or of his attaining the age of 18....

Article 19. (a) The regalia of the crown, including all regalia of the empress and of the crown prince, are inalienable as belonging to the empire. (b) From the date of the proclamation of the present Constitution, all realty registered in the name of the crown are held in trust for the crown under the administration of the emperor and are inalienable. (c) It is the emperor's right to administer all of the inalienable properties of the crown and all profits and revenues therefrom for the benefit of the crown and the empire; and to receive and administer an annual appropriation, as provided by law, from the imperial treasury, which shall, with the aforesaid profits and revenues, be adequate for the fulfilment of his functions.... (d) All properties held in the names of the emperor or members of the imperial family are private property and, as such, are under the same regime as that applicable to all properties of nationals of the empire. (e) The emperor's court shall be under his direction, and he may make such arrangements in regard thereto as he deems appropriate. He may, at will, appoint to, or dismiss from, all posts at his court such persons as he shall see fit.

Article 20. Upon the establishment of a Council of Regency, each member thereof shall take, in the presence of the emperor, the following oath which shall be administered by the archbishop: "In the name of the Almighty, and as a member of the Council of Regency, I hereby swear to defend, with all my power, the rights, privileges and inheritance of his majesty the emperor, so long as I shall remain a member of the Council of Regency; that I will, at all times, respect and defend the constitution; and that in all my actions and conduct, as member of that council, I will ever be motivated by respect for the constitution and the firm resolve of protecting the rights, privileges and inheritance of his majesty the emperor, so that they may be intact at the moment when he shall be anointed and crowned emperor of Ethiopia. So help me God."

The archbishop shall himself take the same oath.

Article 21. On the occasion of his coronation, the emperor shall take the following oath: "In the name of Almighty God, we ... emperor of Ethiopia, swear that we will uphold and defend the constitution of the empire; that we will govern our subjects with patience and devotion to their general welfare and in accordance with the constitution and the laws; that we will faithfully defend, with all the means in our power, the integrity and territory of our empire; that we will faithfully see to the impartial execution of all laws approved by parliament and proclaimed by us; that we profess and will defend the holy orthodox faith based on the doctrines of St. Mark of Alexandria, professed in Ethiopia since the holy emperors Abreha and Atsbiha; that we will ever promote the spiritual and material welfare and advancement of our subjects; and that, with the aid of the Almighty, we will faithfully execute the promises which we have here undertaken. So help us God."

Article 22. On the occasion of the coronation of the emperor, if over 12 years of age, the crown prince or the heir presumptive, as the case may be, all members of the Crown Council and all members of the parliament, shall individually take an oath of homage and fidelity to the emperor.

Article 23. ... The crown prince or the heir presumptive, as the case may be, if over the age of 12 shall take the following oath: "In the name of the Almighty, I hereby swear that I will faithfully observe all the precepts and directions of my august father ('sovereign' in the case of an heir presumptive) and will ever strive to respect his wishes and seek not after that which is not given to me, and not be so impatient as Adonias or so daring as Abeselom; that I will ever conduct myself so as to be worthy of my sire ('sovereign' in the case of an heir presumptive), of my imperial blood and of the high station which is ('may be' in the case of an heir presumptive) my destiny; that I will, at all times, respect the constitution and the laws, and will ever profess and defend the faith of our orthodox church. I swear that, with the assistance of the Almighty, I will faithfully execute the promises which I have here undertaken. So help me God."

Article 24. ... The members of the Crown Council shall take the following oath: "In the name of the Almighty, I hereby swear allegiance and fidelity to my sovereign, his imperial majesty ... and that I will, as member of the Crown Council, faithfully place above all else the interest and welfare of Ethiopia and of its sovereign; that I will, at all times, faithfully respect the constitution and laws of the empire, and that I will disclose no secret or confidential information revealed to me in connection with my official duties and position. So help me God."

Article 25. ... The members of the parliament shall take the following oath: "In the name of the Almighty, I hereby swear allegiance and fidelity to my sovereign, his imperial majesty ... and that I will, as member of the parliament, faithfully place above all else the interest and welfare of Ethiopia and of its sovereign; that I will, at all times, faithfully respect the constitution and laws of the empire, and that I will disclose no secret or confidential information revealed to me in connection with my official duties and position. So help me God."

CHAPTER II—THE POWERS & PREROGATIVES OF THE EMPEROR

Article 26. The sovereignty of the empire is vested in the emperor and the supreme authority over all the affairs of the empire is exercised by him as the head of state, in the manner provided for in the present constitution.

Article 27. The emperor determines the organization, powers and duties of all ministries, executive departments and the administrations of the government and appoints, promotes, transfers, suspends and dismisses the officials of the same.

Article 28. The emperor appoints mayors of the municipalities referred to in Article 129 of the present constitution, from 3 candidates presented, in each case, by the municipal councils thereof.

Article 29. The emperor reserves the right, with the advice and consent of parliament, to declare war. He, further, reserves the right to decide what armed forces shall be maintained.... As commander-in-chief of the armed forces, he has the right to organize and command the said forces; to commission and to confer military rank upon the officers of the said forces; and to promote, transfer or dismiss any of the said officers. He has, further, the right to declare a state of siege, martial law, or a national emergency and to take such measures as are necessary to meet a threat to the defense or integrity of the empire and to assure its defense and integrity.

Article 30. The emperor exercises the supreme direction of the foreign relations of the empire. The emperor accredits and receives ambassadors, ministers and missions; he, alone, has the right to settle disputes with foreign powers by adjudication and other peaceful means, and provides for and agrees to measures of cooperation with foreign powers for the realization of the ends of security and common defense. He, alone, has the right to ratify, on behalf of Ethiopia, treaties and other international agreements and to determine which treaties and international agreements shall be subject to ratification before becoming binding upon the empire. However, all treaties of peace and all treaties and international agreements involving a modification of the territory of the empire, or of sovereignty or jurisdiction over any part of such territory, or laying a burden on Ethiopian subjects personally, or modifying legislation in existence, or requiring expenditures of state funds, or involving loans or monopolies, shall, before becoming binding upon the empire and the inhabitants thereof, be laid before parliament, and if both houses of parliament shall approve the same..., shall then be submitted to the emperor for ratification.

Article 31. (a) The emperor alone confers and withdraws the title of prince and other honors and institutes new orders. (b) Without his special leave, no Ethiopian subject, nor any foreign national in any government service in the empire, may accept any honor, insignia of order, dignity or title of, or from, a foreign government. The granting of any title, honor or order may exempt no one from the common duties and burdens of the subjects, nor may it carry with it any preferential admission to the offices of the state. (c) Officials who are released from office with assurances of imperial favor, retain the title and rank of the office they have filled. (d) The emperor also makes grants from abandoned properties, and properties in escheat, for the purpose of recompensing faithful service to the crown.

Article 32. The emperor has the right to coin, print and issue money.

Article 33. The emperor has the right to convene the annual sessions of the deliberative chambers and to convoke extraordinary sessions thereof. At the opening of each session of the chambers, he may present, or cause to be presented, a speech from the throne concerning the legislative program recommended by him. He has the right to postpone the opening of and to suspend, for not more than 30 days, and to extend, any session of parliament. He has the right to dissolve the chambers, or either of them, by an order providing, at the same time, for the appointment of a new Senate or the election of a new Chamber of Deputies, or both, as the case may be, and for the convocation of the chambers for a session within 4 months from the date of the order.

Article 34. ... The emperor has the right to initiate legislation and to originate other resolutions and to proclaim all laws, after the same shall have been passed by the parliament.

Article 35. The emperor has the right and the duty to maintain justice through the courts and the right to grant pardons and amnesties and to commute penalties.

Article 36. The emperor, as sovereign, has the duty to take all measures that may be necessary to ensure, at all times, the defense and integrity of the empire; the safety and welfare of its inhabitants, including their enjoyment of the human rights and fundamental liberties recognized in the present constitution; and the protection of all his subjects and their rights and interests abroad. Subject to the other provisions of this constitution, he has all the rights and powers necessary for the accomplishment of the ends set out in the present article.

CHAPTER III—RIGHTS & DUTIES OF THE PEOPLE

Article 37. No one shall be denied the equal protection of the laws.

Article 38. There shall be no discrimination amongst Ethiopian subjects with respect to the enjoyment of all civil rights.

Article 39. The law shall determine the conditions of acquisition and loss of Ethiopian nationality and of Ethiopian citizenship.

Article 40. There shall be no interference with the exercise, in accordance with the law, of the rites of any religion or creed by residents of the empire, provided that such rites be not utilized for political purposes or be not prejudicial to public order or morality.

Article 41. Freedom of speech and of the press is guaranteed throughout the empire in accordance with the law.

Article 42. Correspondence shall be subject to no censorship, except in time of declared national emergency.

Article 43. No one within the empire may be deprived of life, liberty or property without due process of law.

Article 44. Everyone has the right ... to own and dispose of property. No one may be deprived of his property except upon a finding by ministerial order issued pursuant to the requirements of a special expropriation law enacted in accordance with the provisions of Articles 88, 89 or 90 of the present constitution, and except upon payment of just compensation determined, in the absence of agreement, by judicial procedures established by law. Said ministerial order, to be effective, shall be approved by the Council of Ministers and published in the *Negarit Gazeta.*

Article 45. Ethiopian subjects shall have the right, in accordance with the conditions prescribed by law, to assemble peaceably and without arms.

Article 46. Freedom to travel within the empire and to change domicile therein is assured to all subjects of the empire....

Article 47. Every Ethiopian subject has the right to engage in any occupation and, to that end, to form or join associations....

Article 48. The Ethiopian family, as the source of the maintenance and development of the empire and the primary basis of education and social harmony, is under the special protection of the law.

Article 49. No Ethiopian subject may be banished from the empire.

Article 50. No Ethiopian subject may be extradited to a foreign country. No other person shall be extradited except as provided by international agreement.

Article 51. No one may be arrested without a warrant issued by a court, except in case of flagrant or serious violation of the law in force. Every arrested person shall be brought before the judicial authority within 48 hours of his arrest. However, if the arrest takes place in a locality which is removed from the court by a distance which can be traversed only on foot in not less than 48 hours, the court shall have discretion to extend the period of 48 hours. The period of detention shall be reckoned as a part of the term of imprisonment imposed by sentence. No one shall be held in prison awaiting trial on a criminal charge the sole penalty for which is a fine.

Article 52. In all criminal prosecutions, the accused, duly submitting to the court, shall have the right to a speedy trial and to be confronted with the witnesses against him, to have compulsory process, in accordance with the law, for obtaining witnesses in his favor, at the expense of the government and to have the assistance of counsel for his defense, who, if the accused is unable to obtain the same by his own efforts or through his own funds, shall be assigned and provided to the accused by the court.

Article 53. No person accused of and arrested for a crime shall be presumed guilty until so proved.

Article 54. Punishment is personal. No one shall be punished except in accordance with the law and after conviction of an offense committed by him.

Article 55. No one shall be punished for any offense which has not been declared by law to be punishable before the commission of such offense, or shall suffer any punishment greater than that which was provided by the law in force at the time of the commission of the offense.

Article 56. No one shall be punished twice for the same offense.

Article 57. No one shall be subjected to cruel and inhuman punishment.

Article 58. No one shall be imprisoned for debt, except in case of legally proved fraud or of refusal either to pay moneys or property adjudged by the court to have been taken in violation of the law, or to pay a fine, or to fulfil legal obligations of maintenance....

Article 59. No sentence of death shall be executed unless it be confirmed by the emperor.

Article 60. Confiscation of property as a penalty shall not be imposed except in cases of treason, as defined by law, against the emperor or the empire; sequestration of property as a penalty shall not be imposed except in cases of property belonging to persons residing abroad and conspiring against or engaging in deliberately hostile acts ... against the emperor or the empire. Attachment proceedings covering the whole or part of the property of a person, made under judicial authority, to cover payment of civil liability, or liability arising out of the commission of an offense, or to meet taxes or fines, shall not be deemed a confiscation of property.

Article 61. All persons and all private domiciles shall be exempt from unlawful searches and seizures.

Article 62. (a) ... No one shall have the right to bring suit against the emperor. (b) Any resident of the empire may bring suit, in the courts of Ethiopia, against the government, or any ministry, department, agency or instrumentality thereof, for wrongful acts resulting in substantial damage. In the event that the courts shall find that such suit has been brought maliciously or without foundation, the government, or any ... instrumentality, or official thereof against whom or which such suit was brought, shall have a right of action against such resident for such malicious or unfounded suit, and the court shall, in such case, decree remedies or penalties according to the law.

Article 63. Everyone in the empire shall have the right to present petitions to the emperor.

Article 64. Everyone in the empire has the duty to respect and obey the constitution, laws, decrees, orders and regulations of the empire. Ethiopian subjects, in addition, owe loyalty to the emperor and to the empire and have the duty of defending the emperor and the empire against all enemies, foreign and domestic, to perform public services, including military services, when called upon to do so, and to exercise the right of suffrage which is conferred upon them by the constitution.

Article 65. Respect for the rights and freedoms of others and the requirements of public order and the general welfare shall alone justify any limitations upon the rights guaranteed in the foregoing articles of the present chapter.

CHAPTER IV—THE MINISTERS OF THE EMPIRE

Article 66. The emperor has the right to select, appoint and dismiss the prime minister and all other ministers and vice ministers, each of whom shall, before entering upon his functions, take before the emperor the following oath of fidelity to the emperor and to the constitution: "In the name of the Almighty, I hereby swear allegiance and fidelity to my sovereign, his imperial majesty ... and that, as member of the Council of Ministers, I will faithfully place above all else the interest and welfare of Ethiopia, and of its sovereign; that I will, at all times, faithfully respect the constitution and laws of the empire, and that I will disclose no secret or confidential information revealed to me in connection with my official duties and position. So help me God."

The appointment, promotion, transfer, suspension, retirement, dismissal and discipline of all other government officials and employes shall be governed by regulations made by the Council of Ministers and approved and proclaimed by the emperor.

Article 67. Princes eligible for the crown shall not be appointed ministers in the Council of Ministers. No one whose parents were not Ethiopian subjects at the time of his birth shall be appointed a minister.

Article 68. Each minister shall be individually responsible to the emperor and to the state for the discharge of the duties of his respective ministry, including the execution of the laws and decrees concerning that ministry.

Article 69. The ministers shall form collectively the Council of Ministers and shall be responsible to the emperor for all advice and recommendations given to him in council. The rules of procedure of the council shall be drawn up by the ministers in council and submitted to the emperor for approval.

Article 70. The emperor may, in such instances as he deems appropriate, convene the Crown Council, which shall consist of the archbishop, such princes, ministers and dignitaries as may be designated by him, and the president of the Senate. The Crown Council shall be presided over by the emperor or by a member designated by him.

Article 71. The ministers shall discuss in council and, through the prime minister, submit to the emperor all matters of policy therein discussed. In all cases in which legislation is deemed to be necessary or appropriate, the decisions made in council and approved by the emperor shall be communicated by the prime minister to parliament in the form of proposals for legislation.

Article 72. The prime minister shall present to parliament proposals of legislation made by the Council of Ministers and approved by the emperor. He shall also present to the emperor the proposals of legislation approved by the parliament and the decrees proposed by the Council of Ministers. He shall have the right to attend any meeting of either chamber of parliament, or any joint meeting of the chambers, or any meeting of any committee of either chamber, and to speak at such meetings on any question under discussion. He shall be obliged to attend personally, or by his deputy, either chamber when his presence is requested by a majority vote of the members thereof and to answer, verbally or in writing, questions concerning his office.

Article 73. The ministers shall have the right to attend any meeting of either chamber of parliament, or any joint meeting of the chambers, or any meeting of any committee of either chamber, and to speak at such meetings on any question concerning the conduct of their ministries; and they shall be obliged, in person, or by their deputies, to answer, verbally or in writing, questions concerning the legislation to be enacted.

Article 74. No minister, nor any person in a position with or in the service of the government may: (a) for remuneration, compensation or benefit of financial value engage in any activity or accept a position in or with any enterprise or organization in which there is no governmental participation; (b) enter into or be a party to any contract or other arrangement with any governmental organization in the empire awarding, permitting or recognizing any concession or monopolistic or other exclusive privilege in the nature of a concession or monopoly. (c) However, such minister or person shall be free to manage and develop his properties so long as their management or development is not prejudicial to or inconsistent with the performance of his duties.

Article 75. The ministers, including the prime minister, may be tried only before the Supreme Imperial Court upon charges of offenses as determined by the law, committed in connection with their official functions. Such prosecution may be initiated either by order of the emperor or by a majority vote of both houses of parliament. A special prosecutor shall be appointed to that end, conformably to the orders of the emperor.

CHAPTER V—THE LEGISLATIVE CHAMBERS

SECTION I—Provisions Applicable to Both Chambers

Article 76. The parliament shall be composed of a Chamber of Deputies and a Senate. No one can be simultaneously a member of both [chambers].... The 2 chambers shall meet together at the beginning and the end of each session ... upon the call of the emperor and upon such other occasions as may be determined by the chambers. The president of the Senate shall preside at all joint meetings of the chambers.

Article 77. The regular sessions of parliament shall convene [annually] on the 23d day of [November] ... in the capital of the empire and shall continue to ... [June 8]. Until a new parliament shall be elected and convened ..., the 2 chambers ..., as heretofore constituted, shall continue to sit and shall ... exercise the prerogatives and functions and fulfil the responsibilities provided for in respect of parliament....

Article 78. No meeting of either chamber of parliament shall be closed to the public except upon a request by the prime minister, or upon a decision by a majority vote of the Chamber of Deputies or the Senate, as the case may be.... No joint meeting of the chambers shall be closed to the public except upon a request by the prime minister or a decision by the majority of each of the chambers.... If, after a question has been declared to be secret, a member of either chamber makes it known to the public, ... he shall be punished according to the provisions of penal law.

Article 79. Neither of the chambers shall commence its deliberations on the first day of any session without the presence of $2/3$ of its members, or continue its deliberations or take any vote on any succeeding day of any session without the presence of a majority of its members. At joint meetings of the chambers, the presence of a majority of the members of each chamber shall be required for deliberations and for voting.

Article 80. If the quorum of deputies and of senators prescribed in Article 79 is not present on the day designated for the convening of parliament or if, thereafter, either of the chambers, or the chambers in joint meeting, cannot continue deliberations or vote for lack of the required attendance, the members present shall take such measures as may be authorized in the rules of procedure of the respective chambers to compel the attendance of a sufficient number of the absent members.

Article 81. Every deputy or senator, before taking his seat in the chamber to which he has been elected or appointed, shall take, before the emperor, or if directed by him, before the president of the legislative chamber concerned, an oath of loyalty to the emperor and to the empire, and shall swear that he will obey the constitution and the laws of the empire and will perform his duties conscientiously and without fear or favor.

Article 82. Each chamber shall determine its own rules of procedure and internal discipline.

Article 83. Members of parliament shall receive salaries determined by law. Any law increasing the salaries of members of parliament shall be effective only from the date of the election of the next parliament.

Article 84. No action or charge may be brought against any member of parliament, or against any minister appearing by right or upon the invitation of either chamber, for words uttered or written statements submitted by him at any meeting of either chamber, or any joint meeting of the chambers, or any meeting of any committee of either chamber. Nevertheless, every member of each chamber of parliament shall be obliged to respect all rules of order, conduct and procedure adopted by such chamber for the transaction of its business and shall be subject to disciplinary action on the part of such chamber for violation of such rules. No action or charge may be brought against any person or any newspaper for publication, by or under the authority of parliament or of either chamber thereof, as the case may be, of any report, paper, votes or proceedings of parliament or either chamber thereof....

Article 85. No member of parliament, during a session thereof, may be arrested or detained or summoned to answer a criminal charge, unless the permission of the chamber of which he is a member be obtained, or he be arrested in *flagrante delicto.* A comparable immunity does not apply to civil cases.

Article 86. Laws may be proposed to either or both chambers of parliament: (a) by the emperor, or (b) by 10 or more members of either chamber of parliament, except that every proposal involving an increase in governmental expenditure or a new or increased tax shall first be presented to the Chamber of Deputies.

Article 87. All matters in either chamber or in joint meetings of the chambers shall be determined by vote of the majority of the members present except as provided in Article 131. In the event of an equal division of votes, the presiding officer shall have a casting vote.

Article 88. Every proposal of legislation approved by one chamber of parliament shall be immediately forwarded through the president thereof to the other chamber. If it is approved by the other, without amendments, within a period of 2 months, it shall be promptly communicated through the prime minister to the emperor and shall either be promulgated as law or returned by the emperor to the chambers with his observations thereon, or with a new proposal of legislation.... All laws duly approved by both chambers of parliament shall be forwarded to the emperor.... In the event that such law shall receive the approval and signature of the emperor, it shall be published by the minister of the pen in the *Negarit Gazeta,* with recital of the affixing of the signature and the great seal of the emperor. All imperial decrees and all ministerial decrees and orders shall be published in the *Negarit Gazeta.*

Article 89. If a proposal of legislation approved by one chamber is not finally acted upon by the other within the aforesaid period of 2 months, the chambers shall meet together to discuss the said proposal. If the proposal is approved in such joint meeting, with or without amendments, within 30 days, it shall be communicated to the emperor for action....

Article 90. If, within the aforesaid period of 2 months, a proposal of legislation approved by one chamber is approved by the other with amendments, the said proposal shall be returned to the first chamber for further consideration. If, upon such further consideration, it is approved, within 30 days, by the first chamber, with the said amendments, it shall be communicated to the emperor for action.... If, within 30 days, the amendments are not accepted by the first chamber, the chambers shall, thereupon, meet together to discuss the proposal. If, in such joint meeting, the proposal is approved, with or without amendments, within 30 days, it shall, thereupon, be communicated to the emperor for action....

Article 91. If a proposal of legislation approved in one of the chambers is rejected by the other within 2 months after its communication to it, ... or if a proposal of legislation is not approved, with or without amendments, after discussion in a joint meeting, ... full reports on the situation shall be promptly communicated to the emperor by the presidents of both chambers of parliament, through the prime minister, and the emperor may, thereupon, cause to be transmitted to both chambers of parliament his observations in regard to such reports and such proposal of legislation, or cause to be transmitted to the chambers a proposal of legislation on the same subject.

Article 92. In cases of emergency that arise when the chambers are not sitting, the emperor may proclaim decrees, consistent with the constitution, which shall have the force of law upon publication in the *Negarit Gazeta,* pending a decision on the same by parliament. To that end, the text of each such decree shall be transmitted for consideration by both chambers of parliament at their first meeting following each such proclamation. In the event that ... parliament shall approve such decrees, they shall continue in force and shall become law upon publication, in the *Negarit Gazeta,* of said approval.

In the event that parliament shall disapprove of any such decree, each such decree shall cease to have force and effect, upon the publication, in the *Negarit Gazeta,* of such disapproval.

SECTION II—The Chamber of Deputies

Article 93. The entire territory of the empire ... shall be divided into electoral districts containing, as nearly as possible, 200,000 inhabitants. The location and limits of each electoral district shall be determined by law, and each such district shall be as regular in shape as circumstances permit. In addition, each town with a population exceeding 30,000 inhabitants shall be entitled to one deputy and an additional deputy for each 50,000 inhabitants in excess of 30,000.

Article 94. Each electoral district shall be represented by 2 deputies.

Article 95. All Ethiopian subjects by birth, of 21 years of age or more, who are regularly domiciled or habitually present in any electoral district and who possess the qualifications required by the electoral law, shall have the right to vote in such electoral district for the candidates from such district, as members of the Chamber of Deputies. The system of voting shall be secret and direct. Details of procedure shall be prescribed by law.

Article 96. To be eligible as a deputy, a person must be, by birth, an Ethiopian subject who: (a) has reached the age of 25 years; (b) is a *bona fide* resident and owner of property in his electoral district, to the extent required by the electoral law; and (c) is not disqualified under any provision of the electoral law.

Article 97. Deputies shall be elected for terms of 4 years and shall be eligible for reelection subject to their continued possession of the qualifications set forth in Article 96.

Article 98. Vacancies that may occur in the membership of the Chamber of Deputies shall be filled as provided in the electoral law.

Article 99. The president and 2 vice presidents of the Chamber of Deputies shall be elected each year from and by the members of the chamber.

Article 100. The Chamber of Deputies shall be sole judge of the qualifications and election of its members.

SECTION III—The Senate

Article 101. The Senate shall consist of the senators appointed by the emperor for 6 years.

Article 102. The Senate shall be composed of a number of persons, not exceeding $\frac{1}{2}$ of the total number of deputies, to be chosen by the emperor from amongst those who have, by their acts, secured the confidence and esteem of the people, and from amongst those who have served their country and their government with distinction.

Article 103. To be eligible for appointment as a member of the Senate, a person must be, by birth, an Ethiopian subject who: (a) has reached the age of 35 years; (b) is a prince or other dignitary, or a former high governmental official, or other person generally esteemed for his character, judgment and public services; and (c) is not disqualified under any provision of the electoral law.

Article 104. The senators first appointed by the emperor ... shall, immediately after their first meeting, be divided into 3 equal groups. The senators of the first group shall be succeeded at the end of the 2d year by senators appointed in accordance with the provisions of Article 101, those of the 2d group, at the end of the 4th year, and those of the 3d group, at the end of the 6th year, so that $\frac{1}{3}$ be succeeded every 2d year.

Article 105. Senators shall be eligible for reappointment subject to their continued possession of the qualifications set forth in Article 103.

Article 106. Vacancies in the membership of the Senate shall be filled by appointments in the manner provided in Article 101.

Article 107. The president and 2 vice presidents of the Senate shall be appointed each year by the emperor from amongst the senators.

CHAPTER VI—THE JUDICIAL POWER

Article 108. The judicial power shall be vested in the courts established by law and shall be exercised by the courts in accordance with the law and in the name of the emperor. Except in situations declared in conformity with the provisions of Article 29 of the present constitution, no persons, except those in active military service, may be subject to trial by military courts.

Article 109. There shall be a Supreme Imperial Court and such other courts as may be authorized or established by law. The jurisdiction of each court shall be determined by law.

Article 110. The judges shall be independent in conducting trials and giving judgments in accordance with the law. In the administration of justice, they submit to no other authority than that of the law.

Article 111. The judges shall be appointed by the emperor. They shall be of the highest character and reputation and shall be experienced and skilled in the law which they may be called upon to apply. Their nomination, appointment, promotion, removal, transfer and retirement shall be determined by special law governing the judiciary.

Article 112. Judges shall sit in public, except that in cases which might endanger public order or affect public morals, they may sit *in camera.*

CHAPTER VII—FINANCE

Article 113. No tax, duty, impost or excise shall be imposed, increased, reduced or abolished, except by law. No exemption from payment of any tax, duty, impost or excise imposed by law shall be granted, except as authorized by law.

Article 114. None of the public revenues shall be expended, except as authorized by law.

Article 115. The fiscal year shall be fixed by special law. The Council of Ministers shall, each year, with the approval of the emperor, and in accordance with the requirements of the law, present to parliament a draft of a law for the approval of the budget of the following year, which budget shall accompany the said draft of law.

Article 116. Each of the chambers of parliament shall examine the said budget in detail and vote on it item by item. Parliament shall [not] . . . increase the total sum set down in the budget for expenditures. The allowance for unforeseen expenses in the said budget shall be fixed by parliament. Parliament shall complete the budget vote for submission to the emperor at least one month before the beginning of the new fiscal year.

Article 117. If the draft of law presented, as provided in Article 116, has not been approved by parliament and proclaimed as law before the beginning of the new fiscal year, the budget of the previous year shall continue in force until a new budget law has been proclaimed.

Article 118. If additional funds are urgently required in the course of any fiscal year, the minister or ministers concerned shall present a supplementary budget to the Council of Ministers, who, with the approval of the emperor, may present an appropriate draft of law to the Chamber of Deputies.

Article 119. No loan or pledge, guaranty or collateral therefor may be contracted for, within or without the empire, by any governmental organization within the empire, except as authorized by a law duly adopted in accordance with the provisions of Articles 88, 89 or 90 of the present constitution.

Article 120. Within 4 months after the end of every fiscal year the Council of Ministers shall present to the emperor and to parliament a detailed report on the receipts and expenditures of the said year. The report shall be immediately referred to the auditor general, who shall, within 3 months, present his comments thereon to the emperor and to parliament.

Article 121. There shall be an auditor general, who shall be appointed by the emperor. He shall be a person who is known to be of the highest character, as well as to possess the requisite technical capacity. His functions shall be defined by law. They shall include the auditing of the accounts of all ministries, departments and agencies of the government and the making of periodical reports to the emperor and to parliament on the fiscal operations of the government. The auditor general shall, at all times, be entitled to have access to all books and records relating to the said accounts.

CHAPTER VIII—GENERAL PROVISIONS

Article 122. The present revised constitution, together with those international treaties, conventions and obligations to which Ethiopia shall be party, shall be the supreme law of the empire, and all future legislation, decrees, orders, judgments, decisions and acts inconsistent therewith shall be null and void.

Article 123. The city of Addis Ababa is the capital of the empire.

Article 124. The flag of the empire consists of 3 horizontal bands, the uppermost green, the middle yellow and the nethermost red....

Article 125. The official language of the empire is Amharic.

Article 126. The Ethiopian Orthodox Church, founded in the 4th century, on the doctrines of Saint Mark, is the established church of the empire and is, as such, supported by the state. The emperor shall always profess the Ethiopian Orthodox faith. The name of the emperor shall be mentioned in all religious services.

Article 127. The organization and secular administration of the established church shall be governed by law. The archbishop and bishops shall be elected by the Ecclesiastical Electoral College, consisting of representatives of the clergy and of the laity of the Ethiopian Orthodox Church. Their spiritual consecration shall be performed according to the canon law, subject to the approval of the emperor of their election and appointment. The emperor has the right to promulgate the decrees, edicts and public regulations of the Church, except those concerning monastic life and other spiritual administrations.

Article 128. No one shall utilize religious activities or organizations for commercial purposes except as authorized by law.

Article 129. Subject to the conditions established by legislation duly adopted in accordance with the provisions of Articles 88, 89 or 90 of the present constitution, all towns shall be incorporated by charters established in accordance with such legislation, and municipal councils shall be established, respectively, in all municipalities of the empire.

Article 130. (a) The natural resources of, and in the sub-soil of, the empire, including those beneath its waters, are state domain. (b) The natural resources in the waters, forests, land, air, lakes, rivers and ports of the empire are a sacred trust for the benefit of present and succeeding generations of the Ethiopian people. The conservation of the said resources is essential for the preservation of the empire. The imperial Ethiopian government shall, accordingly, take all such measures as may be necessary and proper ... for the conservation of the said resources. (c) None of the said resources shall be exploited by any person, natural or juridical, in violation of the principles of conservation established by imperial law. (d) All property not held and possessed in the name of any person, natural or juridical, including all land in escheat, and all abandoned properties, whether real or personal, as well as all products of the sub-soil, all forests and all grazing lands, water-courses, lakes and terrritorial waters, are state domain.

Article 131. The constitution may be amended by an identic joint resolution adopted by ¾ of the members of each chamber in 2 separate sessions of parliament and proclaimed with the approval and authority of the emperor.
Given at Addis Ababa, this 4th day of November 1955.

Haile Selassie I
Emperor

Tsahafe Tezaz Tafarra Worq
Minister of the Pen

Proclamations

4 imperial proclamations were issued by Haile Selassie Nov. 13, 1955:

Under the first proclamation, peasants working farms of up to 40 hectares (98.8 acres) each would receive full title to the land, while those working farms in excess of 40 hectares would receive ownership title to the greater part of their land. Both groups would be exempt from all taxation until 1957.

The 2d proclamation created several agricultural credit banks and abolished the state monopoly for banking. The latter provision enabled foreign banks to open branches in Ethiopia.

A general amnesty was also proclaimed. Prisoners serving sentences of more than 10 years had their terms reduced by 3 years, and those serving life imprisonment had their sentences reduced to 20 years.

The 4th proclamation decreed that education would be free and compulsory for all children 7 to 18.

CONSOLIDATION: 1956-9

A period of political, economic and international consolidation during the years 1956-9 enabled Ethiopia to seat a new parliament, continue the revision of its tax system and strengthen its relations with friendly nations.

Chamber of Deputies Elected

About 2½ million Ethiopians went to the polls Jan. 9-Mar. 9, 1957 to choose 210 members of the Chamber of Deputies from among 597 candidates.

A proclamation providing for the election, as prescribed in the 1955 Constitution, had been issued by Emperor Haile Selassie Aug. 27, 1956. The proclamation, labeled the Chamber of Deputies Electoral Law, scheduled the balloting for the 2-month period in 1957 and provided that "thereafter, general elections shall be held every 4 years on Jan. 9." The law provided for the establishment in the Interior Ministry of a 3-member National Board of Registration & Elections consisting of the interior minister and vice minister plus a 3d person appointed by the emperor.

The electoral law clarified a provision of the 1955 Constitution (Article 96) that a candidate for deputy must be a property owner. The law specified that a candidate must be the "owner of immovable property of a value not less than E$1,000 or of movable property of a value of not less than E$2,000."

The Registration & Elections Board was made responsible for applying and enforcing the electoral law, preparing the procedure for the registration of voters, the presentation of candidates and the holding of the elections.

Registration of prospective voters began Oct. 11, 1956, and about 3½ million of Ethiopia's 20.8 million citizens registered. John Markakis and Asmelash Beyene reported in "Representative Institutions in Ethiopia" (*The Journal of Modern African Studies,* Vol. 5, No. 2, Sept. 1967) that "a very rough estimate puts the number registered at 30% of those eligible to vote." According to Markakis and Beyene: "Widespread ignorance of the purposes of registration and general lack of interest in the election itself were the major factors [for the low rate of registration]. The traditionally oriented folk in the provinces could not readily comprehend the meaning of parliamentary representation, nor did they feel the need for such an institution. Many avoided registration out of fear, spread by rumors, that it was a preliminary step to a new system of taxation or to military conscription. Women abstained heavily, particularly in the Muslim areas. Often, the head of the family, exercising his patriarchal prerogative, registered himself alone. The rate of registration was higher in the cities, and in Addis Ababa it came close to 50% of those eligible. During the voting period, about 2½ million people exercised their newly acquired right, while one million of those who had registered failed to vote."

The electoral board May 9, 1957 began to announce the winners of the E$380-a-month seats in the Chamber of Deputies. Disputed elections delayed the procedure. But 190 deputies, including 2 women, had been confirmed by Nov. 3, when the new chamber met for the first time and the emperor simultaneously nominated a full 35-member Senate. Prime Min. Bitwoded Makonnen Endalkatchaw was appointed president of the Senate and given the title of *ras.*

Taxes & the Economy

The income-tax system was revised under an income tax decree promulgated Sept. 10, 1956. All previous income tax regulations were rescinded, and income taxes were divided into these 3 schedules: (A) taxes on income from employment, (B) taxes on income from rent, lands and buildings used for other than agricultural purposes, and (C) taxes on businessmen and corporations.

Under Schedule A, tax rates ranged from E$.50 monthly on income of E$30 to E$40 a month to E$3 on E$100-E$125-a-month incomes, E$27 on E$500-E$550 incomes, E$90 on E$1,000-E$1,050 incomes, E$210 on E$1,450-E$1,500 incomes and 15% on monthly incomes exceeding E$1,500.

Under Schedule B, which covered income from rent, lands and buildings, rates ranged from 2% on taxable annual incomes of E$360-E$1,500 to 6% on E$4,500-E$6,000 incomes, 9% on E$10,500-E$12,000 and 15% for incomes in excess of E$18,000. The decree provided, however, that "⅓ of the gross income from buildings shall be allowed as a deduction towards repairs and maintenance of buildings and furniture, including the cost of depreciation."

Schedule C set a 15% tax rate on corporations. The rates for businessmen ranged from E$9 for taxable annual incomes of E$360-E$480 to E$335 for E$4,800-E$5,400 incomes, E$1,035 for E$9,600-E$10,200 incomes and 15% for incomes above E$15,000. On both incorporated bodies and individuals a surtax of 10% was charged on income in excess of E$50,000. And a further surtax of 10% was levied on income in excess of E$250,000.

To attract foreign businessmen and investors, the income tax decree allowed representatives of foreign concerns to remain in Ethiopia up to an aggregate of 183 days without paying tax on income received from abroad. Income from the renting of buildings completed after the date of the decree was exempted from the payment of tax for 3 years from the date the building was completed. A new industrial, mining or transport enterprise with invested capital of E$200,000 or more was exempted from tax for 5 years.

A decree proclaimed in Sept. 1956 required "the payment of a federal excise tax on goods manufactured in the Ethiopian empire."

A stamp duty tax proclaimed Oct. 31, 1957 required the payment of stamp duty taxes for promissory notes, contracts, bonds, insurance policies, theater tickets, leases, petitions to government offices and the transfer of motor vehicles.

Decree No. 6 of 1958 established a health tax, which, like the education tax, is collected by the central government and then reallocated to the provinces for local use. The tax is collected at a rate of 30% of the taxes on land.

A salt tax decree of 1959 imposed levies on imported salt and locally produced salt. Salt of 90% purity is taxed at E$8 per 100 kilograms; salt of lower purity is taxed at E$3 to E$5 per 100 kilograms. Exported salt is free of tax.

Decree 37 of 1959 imposed a tobacco tax, which is levied on imported tobacco, matches, cigarette paper and pocket lighters. Wholesalers of such products pay E$40 a year; retailers in urban areas pay E$12 a year, and retailers in other areas E$4 a year.

A series of 5-year plans to improve and modernize the economy was started in 1957. The first 5-year plan, begun in Nov. 1957, was concerned mainly with infrastructure products. (The 2d 5-year plan, started in 1962, was designed to develop industrial and agricultural resources and to improve health and educational services.)

A National Coffee Board, created Oct. 31, 1957, comprised 6 members appointed by the emperor on the recommendation of the ministers of commerce and industry, agriculture, finance and interior. The board's duty is to try to ensure that Ethiopian coffee (the country's primary crop) remains of the "first quality for export." The board was directed to "keep under constant review all legislation dealing with coffee," to "consult the producers, traders and exporters of coffee with a view to ascertaining what legislative steps should be taken to improve the standard of coffee" and "to take such steps as are necessary by educational and experimental schemes to improve the quality of coffee."

Because of the high cost of imported sugar, Ethiopia granted a Dutch firm a concession to start a sugar plantation at Wonji, in the Awash River Valley, near Addis Ababa, and the firm's refinery began production in 1957.

The Koka Dam project near Addis Ababa, put into effect with an allocation of more than E$30 million in an effort to increase the output of electricity, was inaugurated May 31, 1958, and the dam was opened May 4, 1960.

Haile Selassie's Travels

Haile Selassie paid a 3-week visit to India Oct. 25-Nov. 17, 1956 for discussions on world problems and economic, cultural and other relations between Ethiopia and India. One of the results of the conversations was an agreement to build an Indo-Ethiopian textile facility in Ethiopia. (Actual construction was started in 1958, and 2 factories were opened in Akaki and Bahar Dar Apr. 8, 1960.) The emperor met both formally and informally with Indian Pres. Rajendra Prasad, Premier

Jawaharlal Nehru and other Indian officials. While Haile
Selassie was in India, Egypt was invaded by Britain, France
and Israel, and the USSR invaded Hungary. The emperor and
Nehru Nov. 8 issued a joint communique expressing concern at
these "grave and alarming developments in the international
situation, involving violation of human dignity and freedom
and the subjection of peoples by the force of modern arms."

Haile Selassie flew Nov. 17 to Tokyo, where he was
welcomed by Emperor Hirohito, for a 12-day visit to Japan. He
then visited Burma Nov. 29-Dec. 1 before returning to
Ethiopia. His visit to Japan was the first made by a head of
state to Japan since World War II. The emperor was
accompanied during his trip by his 2d son, Makonnen Haile
Selassie, the duke of Harar. (The duke, at the age of 34, was
killed May 12, 1957 in an auto accident near Addis Ababa. The
emperor's 3d son, Prince Sahle Selassie, suffering from a liver
disease, died in Addis Ababa Apr. 21, 1962.)

Haile Selassie made a 2-month tour of Egypt, the Soviet
Union, Czechoslovakia, Belgium, France, Portugal and
Yugoslavia beginning June 24, 1959. After his return to
Ethiopia, the emperor Aug. 29 delivered a report to the nation
in which he said that the purpose of the trip was "to find ways
and means of raising the standard of living of our people and
the economic development of our country; to discuss with
leaders of friendly countries and acquire aid for the
implementation of the program which we have initiated for the
progress of our country; to observe personally their development projects and choose from amongst them those projects
that we believe will aid in the raising of the standard of living
of our people."

During his tour, the emperor visited the USSR June 29-
July 13 and won Soviet agreement to provide a US$100 million
loan for Ethiopian industrial and agricultural development. (A
protocol detailing the Soviet aid was signed Mar. 27, 1960. It
provided that the Soviet Union would build a big oil refinery at
the Red Sea port of Assab [the refinery was opened May 8,
1965], dig a gold mine and build a processing plant for it, survey
Ethiopia for minerals and investigate the posssibility of a
Soviet loan to help build an iron and steel mill in Ethiopia.)

Haile Selassie flew to Prague July 13 for a 4-day visit to Czechoslovakia, where he and Czechoslovak officials discussed proposals for aid to Ethiopia. (The emperor announced Nov. 3 that Ethiopia had accepted an offer of Czechoslovak credits for the development of the Ethiopian economy.)

During a 2-day visit to France July 20-21, Haile Selassie was greeted by Pres. Charles de Gaulle on his arrival in Paris, and the 2 leaders conferred on Ethiopian and French opposition to the formation of either a Muslim-dominated "greater Somalia" or a Pan-African Union led by Ghana and Guinea.

Foreign Relations & Aid

U.S. Vice Pres. Richard M. Nixon, on an 18,000-mile good-will tour of 8 African states, landed in Addis Ababa Mar. 11, 1957 and met with Haile Selassie. Nixon said Mar. 12 that the emperor had indicated "some disappointment" with the U.S. military assistance program for Ethiopia. U.S. State Department officials confirmed in Washington Mar. 12 that Nixon had requested Ethiopian permission for the construction of a U.S. military communications center and port facilities in Massawa, on the Red Sea.

The U.S. International Cooperation Administration reported May 23, 1958 that Ethiopia had been granted economic aid totaling US$2,923,000 in the fiscal year ended June 30, 1956 and US$9,600,000 in the fiscal year ended June 30, 1957. The U.S. shipped 5,000 tons of wheat to Ethiopia Sept. 9, 1958 as emergency drought aid. (Drought and an accompanying famine took about 100,000 lives in Tigre and Wello provinces in 1958-9.)

The establishment of legation-level diplomatic relations between Ethiopia and the Vatican was announced in Addis Ababa Mar. 19, 1957.

The International (World) Bank for Reconstruction & Development lent Ethiopia US$15 million June 21, 1957, for the extension and improvement of the Ethiopian highway system. The agreement provided for the construction of about 530 miles of new roads. The First National City Bank of New York provided $1,491,000 of the loan. The terms: 20 years; 5⅞% interest, including 1% commission; repayment to begin Sept. 1, 1961.

Pres. Tito of Yugoslavia paid a fresh visit to Ethiopia Feb. 1-12, 1959. He was welcomed Feb. 3 by Haile Selassie, who expressed gratitude for Yugoslav aid to Ethiopia. "In the technical and economic aspects," the emperor noted, "Yugoslavia has sent to Ethiopia top-class experts whose cooperation with our experts has shown marvelous results. Similarly in the field of medicine, in economic planning." Some of the Yugoslav aid was being used on the Red Sea port of Assab in Eritrea, on which construction had been started May 10, 1958. After an expenditure by Ethiopia of more than E$26 million and after the receipt of additional aid from Yugoslavia, the port of Assab was opened Dec. 3, 1961.

Under an agreement signed by the German Federal Republic (West Germany) and Ethiopia Apr. 25, 1959, effective July 17, West Germany began a program of providing Ethiopia with books and technical equipment for schools, of helping to recruit German teachers for Ethiopian educational institutions, of sending German experts to prepare reports on the development of Ethiopia's economic resources, and of aiding Ethiopia in the fields of public health and forestry. In return the Ethiopian government agreed not to levy import duties on equipment sent by West Germany or on the personal effects of German experts, and it exempted Germans working in Ethiopia under the program from any personal taxation.

An Ethio-Swedish Clinic for infants and young children, built with Swedish capital, was opened in Addis Ababa Dec. 2, 1959.

Inter-African Affairs

Addis Ababa became an international center in 1958 when a UN Economic Commission for Africa (UNECA) was created with headquarters there. The UN Economic & Social Council had voted unanimously Apr. 29 to establish such a commission to aid "concerted action for the economic development of Africa, including its social aspects." The council May 2 then selected Addis Ababa as the site, and the commission headquarters opened its first meeting in Addis Ababa Dec. 29. UN Secy. Gen. Dag Hammarskjold welcomed the session as "marking the moment when Africa began to assume its full role in the world community."

Ethiopia participated in the first conference of independent African states, which met Apr. 15-22, 1958 in Accra, Ghana. The conferees adopted resolutions pledging (a) common foreign policies based on "nonentanglement" between East and West and (b) support for Algerian rebels in their attempt to gain independence from France. Convened by Ghana Prime Min. Kwame Nkrumah, the conference included representatives of the United Arab Republic, Sudan, Libya, Tunisia, Morocco, Liberia and Ghana.

Representatives of Ethiopia, Liberia, Morocco, Tunisia, Ghana, Guinea, Libya, Sudan and the United Arab Republic met in Monrovia, Liberia Aug. 4-8, 1959 to mobilize support for Algerian independence. They adopted a resolution calling for the withdrawal of French troops from Algeria and demanded that peace negotiations between the 2 parties begin immediately. They also voiced opposition to French plans for nuclear tests in the Sahara.

DEVELOPMENT & SOPHISTICATION: 1960-6

The years 1960-6 were marked by a growing development of Ethiopian institutions and a continuation in the increase in political sophistication. Haile Selassie was challenged in 1960 by a group of civilians and members of his Imperial Body Guard, who unsuccessfully attempted to overthrow him on the ground that he was moving too slowly in his efforts to modernize Ethiopia. Eritrea gave up its federal status in 1962 and became a province of Ethiopia, but Eritrean opponents of this decision rebelled and started a guerrilla movement designed to make Eritrea independent. Farm improvement and industrialization programs, much of this development being assisted by foreign institutions, were emphasized during this period. Under the emperor's guidance, Ethiopia continued to play an increasing role in international affairs. Border disputes, however, remained an undiminished burden.

Attempted Coup Crushed

A revolt against Haile Selassie broke out Dec. 13-14, 1960. The attempted coup, led by Brig. Gen. Mengestu Newaye of the Imperial Body Guard, was suppressed Dec. 16 by troops commanded by Gen. Merid Mengesha.

The revolt was begun while the emperor was abroad on a state visit to Brazil. The 6,000-man Imperial Guard occupied the royal palace, Addis Ababa radio and other key points in the capital under the leadership of Gen. Newaye and his brother, Gov. Germame Newaye of Jigga, a subprovince of Harar Province.

Rebel broadcasts by Addis Ababa radio Dec. 14 proclaimed Haile Selassie's rule at an end and said that Crown Prince Asfa Wossen, 44, had succeeded to the throne. Ras Imru, 68, Selassie's cousin and ex-ambassador to the U.S. and USSR, was named prime minister of a rebel government that pledged a Socialist and nationalist program under a constitutional monarchy. The rebels said they had acted in order to end the alleged feudal autocracy perpetuated in Ethiopia by Haile Selassie.

Army troops commanded by Gen. Mengesha and Maj. Gen. Kebede Gebre attacked the rebel positions in Addis Ababa Dec. 15 after it became clear that most of the army and areas outside the capital remained loyal to Haile Selassie. The pro-Selassie forces reportedly dislodged the rebels and captured most officers of the Imperial Guard by Dec. 16. Maj. Gen. Mulughetta Buli, named army commander by the rebels, was killed by pro-Selassie forces, but the Newaye brothers reportedly escaped. (Germame committed suicide Dec. 24; Mengestu was captured shortly thereafter.)

Haile Selassie flew Dec. 16 from Brazil to Asmara, capital of Eritrea. The next day he entered Addis Ababa, where he was greeted by Crown Prince Asfa Wossen. The emperor, in a radio address Dec. 18, said the crown prince had been forced to cooperate with the rebels but had been exonerated of any role in the coup. He offered amnesty to those rebels who had been misled and who surrendered voluntarily. He denied rebel assertions that his rule had hampered Ethiopia's development.

Haile Selassie said at a news conference Dec. 20 that the rebellion had been "completely crushed" and that he had "no evidence" that any foreign power had been involved. He said that no changes would be made in Ethiopia's government because none were considered necessary and the rebel program of social progress was one "that we have been implementing all the time."

Maj. Assefa Lemma, acting information minister, announced Dec. 21 that Ras Imru had been forced to participate in the rebellion and had been cleared and freed.

Gen. Newaye was convicted by a 3-man tribunal in Addis Ababa Mar. 28, 1961 and was hanged Mar. 31 as a leader in the revolt. The tribunal also sentenced Capt. Kifle Weldemariam to 15 years in prison and Lt. Degefu Tedla to 10 years for their parts in the revolt. (The emperor, Jan. 12 had given a full pardon to all privates and non-commissioned officers of the Imperial Guard.)

The *N.Y. Times* had reported from Addis Ababa Dec. 21, 1960 that more than 1,000 soldiers and civilians had been killed or wounded in the 3-day rebellion. Many ministers had been assassinated by the rebels. Among those assassinated were: Ras Abebe Aregai, minister of defense; Makonnen Habte Wold, minister of commerce and the interior; Ras Seyoum Mangasha, governor general of Tigre Province; Blatta Dawit Okbagzy, minister of state in the Foreign Affairs Ministry; Tadessa Negash, minister of state in the Justice Ministry; Eshete Geda, vice minister of the interior; Abdullahai Mumie, vice minister of finance; Kebret Astatkie, assistant minister of the interior; Gebre-Wold Ingeda Worq, minister of state in the Ministry of the Pen; Lemma Wolde Gabriel, Letibellu Gebre and Blatta Ayele Begre.

Many civilians who had sympathized with the rebel leaders were removed from their government positions by Haile Selassie. But ministers who had remained loyal to the emperor found that the coup did indeed have an impact. Haile Selassie, in an attempt to bind together opponents of the regime, which included students, army officers, young officials and labor leaders, agreed to modernize at a faster rate than in the past. "We have recognized and followed," the emperor said Apr. 14, 1961. Robert Hess asserted in "Ethiopia" (*National Unity and Regionalism in Eight African States*) that, since 1960, in many areas of policy making "the emperor now follows rather than directs the tide of modernization."

Local Government Reform Effort Fails

Haile Selassie May 24, 1962 unsuccessfully attempted a wide-ranging reform of local government in Ethiopia. His draft Proclamation to Establish Self-Governmment in the Empire of Ethiopia, which did not become law, attempted to alter completely the administration of the provinces as established by Decree No. 1 of 1942. It met with strong opposition in parliament.

The draft proclamation, published by the Imperial Ethiopian Institute of Public Administration, would have given autonomous powers to the subprovinces and provinces in numerous issues of substance. A council consisting of one representative from each subdistrict or 3 representatives from each district would have been created in each subprovince.

These representatives would have been elected by popular vote of their district or subdistrict to serve 6-year terms. The council would have assumed power over education, road construction and hospitals. $\frac{3}{4}$ of the members of a council, by affirmative vote in 2 separate sessions, would have been empowered to adopt "a statement of no-confidence in the governor." The draft proclamation would have authorized the imposition by the councils of "additional taxes," if needed, but the finance minister would have been required to "issue regulations on the levying of such taxes." By providing a fixed term in office and granting autonomy to local officials, the emperor seemed to be sanctioning a devolvement of some of his power.

For 4 years nothing was heard publicly of the draft proclamation. Then Local Self-Administration Order No. 43 was published Mar. 14, 1966. This order was a weakened version of the 1962 draft proclamation. Under Order No. 43, the councils had no right to remove a governor or to impose additional taxes unilaterally. The term of office for council members was reduced to 4 years. Membership on a council was increased to 7 representatives.

When parliament reconvened in 1967, however, it rejected the 1966 order and forced the executive branch to continue to adhere to Decree No. 1 of 1942. This ended the attempt to decentralize local administration.

In the parliamentary debate, many reasons were given for voting against the order. This major reason indicates why the traditional power groups opposed the emperor: "While it is clear that Ethiopia has existed for the last 3,000 years ... it is also known that [Ethiopia] is composed of different tribal groups which were far from regarding one another as members of the same nation, viewing each other as outsiders, having different outlooks and with no free intermingling; and to create separate and autonomous *awrajas* [subprovinces] before the people know one another ... would be encouraging separatist tendencies."

Members of a joint committee of the Chamber of Deputies and the Senate severely criticized the executive branch for offering the self-administration order: "That rural areas do not have any development projects is clear to anyone as they have not enjoyed educational, health, transportation and other services. The minister of interior, together with other concerned ministers, could have ... given these areas chance for development with the taxes estimated for these purposes without creating a dual administrative system suggested by the proclamation."

(The security police announced Nov. 26, 1966 the arrest of several Galla "dissidents" on charges of conspiring against the government. The police reported that Brig. Gen. Gaddesse Biru, ex-deputy commander of the territorial army, had been captured by villagers. One of the alleged plotters was identified by the police as Lt. Mammo Mazemoir, who was charged with throwing 2 hand-grenades into an Addis Ababa cinema 8 days previously. 36 persons, including several Americans and other foreigners, had been injured.)

Elections & Cabinets

Ethiopia's 2d Chamber of Deputies election took place Jan. 9, 1961, and nearly 4 million of the 4½ million Ethiopians who registered actually cast their ballots. They elected 210 deputies from among 940 candidates.

Emperor Haile Selassie chose Aklilou Habte Wold as prime minister to head a new cabinet, whose composition, as made public Apr. 17, 1961, was: Foreign Affairs Minister—ex-Amb.-to-U.S. Ras Mikael Imru; Interior—Lt. Gen. Abiye Abebe; Defense—Lt. Gen. Merid Mengesha; Finance—Yilma Deressa; Justice—Djejazmatch Uawde Gabre Selassie; Commerce & Industry—Endalkachew Makonnen; National Community Development—Col. Tamrat Yiggezu; Education—Haddis Alemayehu; Public Works & Communications—Mahteme Selassie Wolde Meskel; Posts, Telegraphs & Telephones—Emanuel Abraham; Health—Abebe Retta; Pensions & Supplies—Uawde Balaineh; Information—Ghirmatchew Tekle Hawariat; Imperial Court—Tafara Worq Kidane Wold; Vice Minister of the Pen—Ketema Yifru; Vice Minister of Mines & State Domains—Fitawrari Haile Mikael Uawde; Agriculture Vice Minister—Tadesse Yacob.

For the election of Jan. 9, 1965, the number of registered voters rose to 5,137,157 of the approximately 27 million citizens. The number of people actually voting, however, declined to 3,203,113. The Chamber of Deputies had been enlarged, so 250 deputies were chosen from the 1,308 candidates. The victors also received an increase in salary, which was almost doubled—from the original E$380 a month to E$750.

Haile Selassie Mar. 23, 1966 promulgated a decree delegating to the prime minister the emperor's power to appoint cabinet members. The decree provided that the cabinet would be collectively responsible to the emperor and parliament.

Prime Min. Aklilou Habte Wold Apr. 11 reorganized the cabinet and added 5 new ministries—for Planning & Development, Land Reform, Public Works, Communications, and Information & Tourism. Habte Wold retained his post as prime minister and took the 2 additional ministries of interior and the pen.

The other assignments were: Defense—Lt. Gen. Merid Mengesha; Imperial Court—Tafara Worq Kidane Wold; Finance—Yilma Deressa; Foreign Affairs—Ketema Yifru; Commerce & Industry—Abebe Retta; Community Development & Social Affairs—Getahun Tessema; Education—Akale-Worq Habte Wold; Communications—Emanuel Abraham; Public Health—Asfaha Wolde Mikael; Agriculture—Ghirmatchew Tekle Hawariat; Planning & Development—Haddis Alemayehu; Justice—Mammo Tadesse; Mines—Maj. Assefa Lemma; chief of staff of territorial army (with rank of minister)—Dejazmatch Kebede Tessema; chief of public security (with rank of minister)—Kifle Ergetu; high commissioner of Central Personnel Agency and commissioner of Pension Board (with rank of minister)—Tadesse Yacob.

These 6 ministers of state were also cabinet members: Abdurahman Sheh—minister of state in the Interior Ministry; Seyoum Haregot—minister of state in the prime minister's office; Belete Gebre Tsadik—minister of state for land reform and administration; Dr. Haile Giorgis Workineh—minister of state for public works; Minassie Haile—minister of state for information and tourism; Salah Hinit—minister of state for posts and telegraphs. Ex-Commerce & Industry Min. Endalkachew Makonnen was appointed permanent Ethiopian representative at the UN with the rank of minister.

Haile Selassie appointed Maj. Gen. Kebede Gebre to be defense minister Dec. 5, 1966 to replace Gen. Merid Mengesha, who had died Sept. 10. Kifle Ergetu was simultaneously appointed interior minister. Gen. Kebede, who served in the

Ethiopian army contingent in Korea, had been deputy governor general of Harar Province.

Eritrea Becomes a Province

The Ethiopian parliament and Eritrean Assembly voted unanimously Nov. 14, 1962 to end Eritrea's status and to unite Eritrea with Ethiopia as a province. The Assembly declared that the federation had caused misunderstanding between the 2 countries.

Haile Selassie announced that the change would take place immediately. After the unification of the 2 nations, the emperor said in a statement Nov. 16: "The people of Eritrea have repeatedly requested us to abolish the federal system and reestablish a unitary form of administration. Federation contained inherent dangers of creating misunderstanding among the people and furthermore created a duplication of administrative apparatus."

The change in Eritrea's status, however, was opposed by many Eritrean political figures and students. About 100 Eritrean students stoned the Ethiopian embassy in Cairo Nov. 17 in protest against the change. Ethiopian Amb.-to-Egypt Mikael Malak Andoum shot and wounded 2 students and an Egyptian policeman during the riot outside the embassy.

The Eritrean Liberation Front (ELF), a Muslim action group organized in 1958 in Cairo, formed a "liberation army" shortly after Eritrea became an Ethiopian province. The front's goal was the liberation of Eritrea from Ethiopia. The front's strength was never made public (although by 1970 it was estimated that some 2,000 members were under arms). The Sudanese government reported June 6, 1965 that it had found 18 tons of Czech arms on Sudanese territory intended for Eritrean rebels against Ethiopia. Activities of the ELF's "liberation army" were never made clear, but some ELF members had received asylum in Syria, and Damascus radio Nov. 10, 1966 broadcast an ELF "military communique" claiming that the "Eritrean liberation army" had scored victories against Ethiopian military units in Eritrea in October.

The Economy

A major success in Ethiopia's economic program was the growth of the coffee industry, which accounted for about half of the nation's exports. Ethiopian coffee exports rose from 35,670 tons in the 1958-9 season to 52,885 in 1959-60, to 55,160 in 1960-1, to 59,885 in 1961-2, to 68,535 in 1962-3 and to a record 75,642 in 1963-4.

A variety of individual projects and enterprises were in various stages of progress:

● The Addis Ababa Commercial Bank was incorporated July 2, 1963. This was the first bank formed under the 1962 Banking Law amendment, which authorized the creation of banks other than the Ethiopian State Bank.

● The construction of Ethiopia's first pulp and paper mill, an US$8 million facility, was started under an agreement, announced July 12, 1963, by the U.S. firm Parsons & Whittemore and the Commerce & Industry Ministry.

● A national TV service was started in Addis Ababa Nov. 2, 1964. The capital then had about 1,000 TV sets.

● A project to develop a viable market and business center in Soddo (located in Wollamo subprovince of Sidamo Province) was started in 1964. It was financed largely by funds from the Soddo district. These contributions totaled approximately US$200,000 a year and were collected as an additional land tax of about 30%. The project provided for the expansion of shopping areas, the building of government offices and the planning of industries. Monthly meetings were held in Soddo, where administrators, merchants and resident representatives of technical ministries discussed economic problems. The program had been planned by the district governor, several Israeli advisers and the emperor, who donated US$75,000 in government funds to the project. Some 370 families were permanently resettled in the district during 1964-7, and each family received 5 hectares of land. Cotton and tobacco were introduced, and initial high yields were reported.

● The laying of water pipelines for the city of Harar was started under an agreement between the Ethiopian Interior Ministry and Solel Boneh Overseas and Harbour Works Co., Ltd., both of Israel. The contract, announced in Mar. 1965, provided for the expenditure of about E$1½ million to lay nearly 15 kilometers of steel pipeline from Lake Alemaya to Harar. (Solel Boneh had previously handled such Ethiopian projects as the construction of the Jimma-Agaro road and the Addis Zemen-Bahr-Dar road as well as construction at Bole Airport, Addis Ababa.)

● The collaboration of Duncan Brothers of Calcutta in the erection of a plastics processing plant in Ethiopia was reported Aug. 5, 1965 to have received Indian government approval. The Indian company agreed to take 30% of the stock of a new Ethiopian company created to run the plant. The Indian contribution was in the form of plant and building materials, and Indian personnel were to manage the new company for 15 years.

● A new Ethiopian shipping company, the Ethiopian Trans-Atlantic Shipping Line, was formed in May 1966, with Canadian cooperation, to transport freight between Ethiopia and North America. It was started with capital of US$100,000.

● Haile Selassie inaugurated a US$2 million synthetic textile plant Dec. 24, 1966 at Mojo, 50 miles east of Addis Ababa. The factory, with an annual capacity of 3¼ million yards of nylon products, was considered capable of satisfying Ethiopia's domestic needs.

● The government-owned Ethiopian Airlines observed its 20th anniversary in Dec. 1966. It was operating 26 planes, including 3 Boeing 720B jets, over routes totaling 50,000 miles. In 1966 it netted US$1.2 million on revenues of US$20 million.

The gross national product in this period rose from E$2,351,800,000 in 1961 to E$2,430,100,000 in 1962, E$2,538,600,000 in 1963, E$2,891,900,000 in 1964, E$3,307,800,000 in 1965 and E$3,484,500,000 in 1966.

The value of imports continued to exceed the value of exports during the period. Imports, exports and balance-of-trade totals since shortly after the end of World War II (in millions of Ethiopian dollars):

Balance of Trade		Imports	Exports
1946	− 18-7	94-9	76-2
1947	− 22-5	121-2	98-7
1948	− 27-4	124-0	96-6
1949	− 25-1	119-1	94-0
1950	− 14-2	105-5	91-3

Balance of Trade		Imports	Exports
1951	+ 4-5	147-4	151-9
1952	− 30-5	161-9	131-4
1953	+ 31-5	137-9	169-4
1954	+ 0-2	160-1	160-3
1955	− 5-8	168-0	162-2
1956	− 5-7	157-1	151-4
1957	+ 13-6	178-4	192-0
1958	− 36-8	193-6	156-8
1959	− 29-7	208-9	179-2
1960	− 26-7	219-3	192-6
1961	− 46-9	235-6	188-7
1962	− 57-8	257-3	199-5
1963	− 52-7	276-1	223-4
1964	− 45-1	307-6	262-5
1965	− 85-9	375-7	289-8
1966	−126-8	404-3	277-5

Production of major crops in this period (in thousands of tons)

Fiscal Year	Coffee	Barley	Maize	Sorghum	Vegetables, Fruits & Spices
1962-3	132.7	774.0	695.0	1,100.0	1,604.3
1963-4	139.1	785.7	713.9	1,121.0	1,682.6
1964-5	170.4	804.8	727.2	1,134.0	1,713.8
1965-6	140.0	821.7	755.5	1,165.2	1,843.7

The gross value of industrial production in Ethiopia rose from a total of E$176½ million in fiscal 1963-4 to E$219,729,000 in 1964-5 and E$269,822,000 in 1965-6. The value of food-industry output in this period rose from E$59.9 million to E$72,309,000 in 1964-5 and E$80,912,000 in 1965-6. Textile output declined slightly from E$63 million in 1963-4 to E$62,570,000 in 1964-5 and then increased to E$79,082,000 in 1965-6. Beverage industry output rose from E$23 million to E$36,665,000 in 1964-5 and E$41,954,000 in 1965-6. The value of hides and skins output rose from E$6 million to E$9,140,000 in 1964-5 and E$13,074,000 in 1965-6. Construction industry production increased from E$5,200,000 to E$10,653,000 in 1964-5 and E$12,668,000 in 1965-6.

Tax System Updated

A fresh revision of the income tax system was instituted in Proclamation No. 173 of June 2, 1961. All previous income tax laws were rescinded, and the new law raised the amount of tax to be paid. Rates were set under 3 schedules:

Under Schedule A, tax on income from employment "is charged and collected monthly [from income] including, without limitations, salaries, wages, allowances, pensions, director's fees, and other personal emoluments." The tax on income from employment was actually imposed on the income of the preceding month. Rates ranged from E$.75 on incomes of E$30 to E$40 a month to E$3.75 on E$80-E$100 incomes, E$27 on E$400-E$450 incomes, E$60 on E$650-E$700 incomes, 10% on E$750-E$800 incomes, 13% on E$1,000-E$1,075 incomes, 20% on E$4,375-E$5,000 incomes and 21% for everything above E$5,000.

Schedule B, covering "tax on income from rent of lands and buildings used for other than agricultural purposes," imposed rates ranging from 2% on E$360-E$390 annual incomes to 6% on E$4,500-E$6,000 incomes, 10% on E$9,600-E$10,800 incomes, 15% on E$14,400-E$15,000 incomes and 16% on all above E$15,000. In addition, a surtax of 10% was levied "on any part of the income which is in excess of E$30,000." Deductions for the cost of repairs and maintenance for and the depreciation of buildings, furniture and equipment were permitted.

Schedule C covered "tax on income from business, from professional and vocational occupations, from the exploitation of woods and forests for lumbering purposes and for all other sources not elsewhere mentioned herein." Such businesses were taxed at the rate of 16% of profits, and individuals engaged in them were taxed at rates ranging from E$10 on incomes of E$360-E$480 a year to E$57 on E$1,200-E$1,500, E$216 on E$3,000-E$3,600 incomes, E$720 on E$9,000-E$9,600 incomes, 10% on E$10,800-E$11,400 incomes and 15% on incomes of E$13,800 to E$15,000. A surtax of 10% was levied on taxable income in excess of E$30,000, and an additional surtax of 10% was imposed on taxable income in excess of E$150,000. However: "In the case of a body incorporated in Ethiopia having a paid-up capital of E$5 million or more, the limits for assessing the surtaxes set forth shall be increased by multiplying the limits of said surtaxes (E$30,000 and E$150,000, respectively) by the coefficient equal to $\frac{1}{4}$ of the number of complete millions of Ethiopian dollars of paid-up capital."

Exemptions were provided for (1) income from agriculture, (2) income received by unskilled day workers, (3) interest from bank accounts and (4) income received by foreigners representing foreign businesses who do not remain in Ethiopia for 183 days in the aggregate. Industries investing more than E\$200,000 before the commencement of operations were exempted from income tax for 5 years. Industries investing additional capital of more than E\$500,000 to extend their enterprises may be granted exemptions on the income derived from the extensions for up to 5 years. Income from the leasing of new buildings was exempted for 3 years.

This editor noted in "The Tax System of Ethiopia" (*The American Journal of Economics and Sociology,* Vol. 29, No. 1, Jan. 1970), in reference to the 1961 Income Tax Proclamation: "... Ethiopia, while trying to encourage foreign investment, loses revenue by allowing substantial exemptions to that investment. In addition to losses sustained by the above exemptions, it is estimated that, at most, only 75% of income taxes in Schedules A, B and C is ever collected.... The outright refusal by some to pay and the inefficiency within ... the Ministry of Finance account for some of the loss. However, the politics of landlordism is involved, and in this matter the modern political system must bow to the traditional ascriptive norms of Ethiopian politics. Collection is hampered also by the failure of employes to report that they have more than one employer. They thus avoid paying a percentage of their taxes. This practice continues because ... too much flexibility exists in the income reporting and accounting procedure. As a result, out of a population of some 22 million people, income tax revenue in FY [fiscal year] 1965/66 amounted to only E\$33.8 million."

A transaction tax—on sales—was proclaimed in 1963. Under regulations published Jan. 30, 1964, this new tax combined revenues from a tax on goods manufactured locally (5%), a turnover tax and a tax on all construction work. Because of a conflict with other tax laws, certain exemptions were made. Deductions in the amounts of excise taxes were permitted for alcohol, sugar, cotton goods, yarn, salt and tobacco if manufactured locally. Locally manufactured ice cream, coffee, tires, tailored suits and dresses were also exempted. The regulations required that "every trader shall pay the turnover tax on all sales made by him." Since the accounts were kept by the traders themselves without any meaningful governmental supervision, however, collections were not efficient. The rate on manufactured items was 1% of sales, paid quarterly. The rate on construction work was 2% of the cost of the work. The total revenue from the transaction tax in fiscal 1965-6 was E$37.8 million.

Additional excise taxes were proclaimed July 13 and July 16, 1965. The 3 basic items taxed were sugar, yarn and textiles. The sugar tax was E$15 per 100 kilograms. The yarn tax was E$.15 a kilogram, and the textile tax was E$.35 a kilogram.

A tax on alcohol was proclaimed Apr. 22, 1965. Total revenue from the alcohol tax in fiscal 1965-6 amounted to some E$17 million, or 5% of the total ordinary revenue, compared with 1.5% of the ordinary revenue produced by land tax. There were no exceptions to the alcohol tax except for homemade *tej* and *talla,* traditional and popular Ethiopian drinks. The levies included an annual excise license for domestic manufacturers; E$500 was levied for a distillery of alcohol, E$200 for the production of alcoholic liquor and lesser amounts for the production of beer, stout and perfumes and for *tej* and *talla* manufactured in factories.

African Unity

Emperor Haile Selassie and Ethiopia played an increasingly important role in African affairs and in international relations in general during the 1960s. Ethiopia's capital, Addis Ababa, was used frequently as the site of international meetings, and it ultimately became the site of the headquarters of the new, continent-wide Organization of African Unity.

The 2d conference of independent African states took place June 14-24, 1960 in Addis Ababa. Haile Selassie opened the conference by urging the creation of an African development bank and other joint economic and political measures for African unity. A resolution adopted by the conferees urged all participating governments to join in trade sanctions against South Africa. Other resolutions approved at the conference expressed "indignation" at South Africa's "shameful policy" of "racial discrimination." They urged member states to (1) sever all trade and diplomatic relations with South Africa and (2) bar South African shipping from their ports and planes from their airfields. The conference was attended by delegations from 11 independent African states: Cameroon, Ethiopia, Ghana (Haile

Selassie toured Ghana Dec. 1-5, 1960), Guinea, Liberia, Libya, Morocco, Nigeria, Sudan, Tunisia and the UAR (United Arab Republic). Togo and the Congo Republic did not attend. Observer delegations were sent by several non-independent African states: Kenya, the Mali Federation of Senegal & Sudan, the Belgian Congo, Malagasy and Portuguese Angola.

Haile Selassie represented Ethiopia at the conference of independent African states held in Lagos, Nigeria Jan. 25-30, 1962. 19 independent African countries sent delegations. Haile Selassie, in an address at the conference, suggested that a committee be set up to draft plans for an Organization of African States, which would provide the medium for the peaceful settlement of inter-African disputes. He said: "We are told that Africa has been split into competing groups and that this is inhibiting cooperation among the African states and severely retarding African progress.... Ethiopia considers herself a member of one group only—the African group... When we Africans have been misled into pigeonholing one another, into attributing rigid and inflexible views to states which were present at one conference but not at another, then we shall, without reason or justification, have limited our freedom of action and rendered immeasurably more difficult the task of joining our efforts, in harmony and brotherhood, in the common cause of Africa.... No wide and unbridgeable gulf exists between the various groupings which have been created. It is our belief, on the contrary, that a close and careful analysis of the policies adopted by the African nations on a wide range of questions emphasizes, not the differences among them, but the large number of views which they share in common.... It would be remarkable indeed did 28 nations, in their policies and programs, reveal no divergencies of opinion. We may take satisfaction and encouragement from the fact that such a large measure of identity of approach and attitude already exists. We urge that this conference use this as its starting point, that we emphasize and lay stress on the areas of similarity and agreement rather than ... disagreements ... among us."

Haile Selassie and Pres. Sekou Toure of Guinea discussed the problems of African unity during a visit of the latter to Addis Ababa June 22-24, 1962.

Haile Selassie met with the heads of 29 other African states in Addis Ababa May 22-25, 1963 in an extraordinary conference that closed with the signing of the charter for what became the Organization of African Unity (OAU). The conferees agreed to establish the OAU's headquarters in Addis Ababa.* This was the biggest meeting of heads of African states ever held. In addition to the emperor, national leaders at the conference were: Ahmed Ben Bella (of Algeria); Ahmadou Ahidjo (Cameroon); David Dacko (Central African Republic); Francois Tombalbaye (Chad); Joseph Kasavubu (Congo-Leopoldville); Abbe Fulbert Youlou (Congo-Brazzaville); Hubert Maga (Dahomey); Leon M'ba (Gabon); Kwame Nkrumah (Ghana); Sekou Toure (Guinea); Felix Houphouet-Boigny (Ivory Coast); William V. S. Tubman (Liberia); Modibo Keita (Mali); Mokhtar Ould Daddah (Mauritania); Hamani Diori (Niger); Sir Abubakar Tafawa Balewa (Nigeria); Leopold S. Senghor (Senegal); Adan Abdullah Osman (Somalia); Philibert Tsiranana (Malagasy); Gen. Ibrahim Abboud (Sudan); Julius K. Nyerere (Tanganyika); Habib Bourguiba (Tunisia); Habemenshi (Rwanda); Sir Milton Margai (Sierre Leone); Milton Obote (Uganda); Gamal Abdel Nasser (United Arab Republic); King Mwambudsa IV (Burundi); Crown Prince Hassan Mohammed Rida (Libya); Maurice Yameogo (Upper Volta).

Haile Selassie was elected honorary president of the conference May 22. In his opening address he said:

> We are meeting here today to lay the basis for African unity. Let us, here and now, agree upon the basic instrument which will constitute the foundation for the future growth ... of this continent.

> Africa is today in mid-course, in transition from the Africa of yesterday to the Africa of tomorrow.... The task on which we have embarked—the making of Africa—will not wait. We must act to shape and mold the future and leave our imprint on events as they pass into history. We seek at this meeting to determine whether we are going to chart the course of our destiny. It is no less important that we know whence we came. An awareness of our past is essential to the establishment of our personality and our identity as Africans.

> This world was not created piecemeal. Africa was born no later and no earlier than any other geographical area on this globe. Africans, no more and no less than other men, possess all human attributes, talents and deficiencies, virtues and faults. Thousands of years ago civilizations flourished in Africa.... Africans were politically free and economically independent. Their social patterns were their own and their cultures truly indigenous. The obscurity which enshrouds the centuries which elapsed between those earlier days and the rediscovery of Africa is being dispersed.... Men in other parts of this earth occupied themselves with their own concerns and, in their

---

*Ethiopia provided the building and staff for the provisional OAU secretariat and defrayed its costs for 2 years.

conceit, proclaimed that the world began and ended at their horizons. All unknown to them, Africa developed in its own pattern, growing in its own life, and in the 19th century finally re-emerging into the world's consciousness. . . .

The period of colonialism into which we were plunged culminated with our continent fettered and bound, with our once proud and free peoples reduced to humiliation and slavery, with Africa's terrain checker-boarded by artificial and arbitrary boundaries. . . . Africa was a physical resource to be exploited, and Africans were chattels to be purchased bodily, or at best peoples to be reduced to vasselage and lackeyhood. Africa was the market for the produce of other nations and the source of the raw materials with which their factories were fed. Today Africa has emerged from this dark passage. . . . Africa has been reborn as a free continent and Africans have been reborn as free men. . . .

Africa's victory . . . is not yet total, and areas of resistance still remain. Today we name as our first great task the final liberation of those Africans still dominated by foreign exploitation and control. . . . We must make one final supreme effort. . . . Our liberty is meaningless unless all Africans are free. Our brothers in the Rhodesias, Mozambique and Angola as well as in South Africa cry out in anguish for our support and assistance. We must align and identify ourselves with all aspects of their struggle. . . .

Let us also resolve that old wounds shall be healed and past scars forgotten. It was thus that Ethiopia treated the invader nearly 25 years ago, and Ethiopians found peace with honor in this course. . . . We must live in peace with our former colonizers, shunning recrimination and bitterness and forswearing the luxury of vengeance and retaliation lest the acid of hatred erode our souls and poison our hearts. . . . Our efforts as free men must be to establish new relationships, devoid of any resentment and hostility, and restore our belief and faith in ourselves as individuals, dealing on a basis of equality with other equally free peoples. . . .

We look to the vision of an Africa not merely free but united. . . . We know that there are differences among us. . . . But we also know that unity can be and has been attained among men of the most disparate origins, that differences of race, religion, culture, and tradition are no insuperable obstacle to the coming together of peoples. . . . We are determined to create a union of Africans. . . . It is our duty and privilege to rouse the slumbering giant of Africa—not to the nationalism of Europe of the 19th century, not to regional consciousness, but to the vision of a single African brotherhood bending its united efforts towards the achievement of a greater and nobler goal.

Above all, we must avoid the pitfalls of tribalism. If we are divided among ourselves on tribal lines we open our doors to foreign intervention and its potential harmful consequences. . . . But while we agree that the ultimate destiny of this continent lies in political union, we must at the same time recognize that the obstacles to be overcome in its achievement are numerous and formidable. Africa's peoples did not emerge into liberty in uniform conditions. Africans maintain different political systems; our economies are diverse; our social orders are rooted in differing cultures and traditions. Further, no clear consensus exists on the 'how' and the 'what' of this union. Is it to be federal, confederal, or unitary? Is the sovereignty of individual states to be reduced, and, if so, by how much and in what areas? On these and other

questions there is no agreement; and if we wait for agreed answers generations hence matters will be little advanced, while the debate still rages.

We should therefore not be concerned that complete union is not attained
from one day to the next. The union we seek can only come gradually as the
day-to-day progress which we achieve carries us slowly but inexorably along
this course.... Thus a period of transition is inevitable. Old relations and
arrangements may for a time linger. Regional organizations may fulfil
legitimate functions and needs which cannot yet be otherwise satisfied, but
the difference is that we recognize these circumstances for what they are—
temporary expedients designed to serve only until we have established the
conditions which will bring total African unity within our reach.

There is, nonetheless, much that we can do to speed this transition.... There
are issues on which we stand united and questions on which there is
unanimity of opinion. Let us seize on these areas of agreement and'... take
action now which, while taking account of present realities, nonetheless
constitutes clear and unmistakable progress along the course plotted out for
us by destiny....

What we still lack ... is the mechanism which will enable us to speak with
one voice when we wish to do so and to implement decisions on African problems when we are so minded. The commentators of 1963 speak ... of the
Monrovia States, the Brazzaville Group, the Casablanca Powers, and many
more. Let us put an end to these terms. What we require is a single African
organization ... which will facilitate acceptable solutions to disputes among
Africans and promote the study and adoption of measures for common
defense and programs for cooperation in the economic and social fields....

We personally, who have throughout our lifetime been ever guided and
inspired by the principle of collective security, would not now propose
measures which depart from or are inconsistent with this ideal or with the
declaration of the UN Charter.... It would be worse than folly to weaken
the one effective world organization which exists today.... The African
organization which we envisage is not intended in any way to replace in our
national or international life the position which the United Nations has
earned and rightfully occupies....

If we succeed in the tasks which lie before us, our names will be remembered
and our deeds recalled by those who follow us. If we fail, history will wonder
at our failure and mourn what was lost.

Haile Selassie officiated at the opening of OAU headquarters (on a site donated by Ethiopia in Addis Ababa) Oct. 7,
1965. He called the OAU the "most important organ for peace
and progress ever devised in the continent of Africa." Haile
Selassie said: "It is fitting that we should again today reaffirm
Ethiopia's unswerving support to OAU. We, personally, and
our people shall devote all efforts and energies to the growth of
OAU and the principles for which it stands."

Opening the 7th session of the OAU Council of Ministers
in Addis Ababa in Nov. 1966, Haile Selassie said: "Those forces
that undermine African independence and unity are continuing
their attempts to sow the seeds of discord amongst Africans.

There are elements bent upon jeopardizing our political, economic and social institutions. We must confront these difficulties with courage.... Unity of effort is indispensable if we are to surmount our problems in this regard.... The ... decolonization of our continent is not yet completed, and, therefore, it becomes all the more incumbent upon us to rededicate ourselves to accelerate the irreversible trend of total emancipation of Africa. The people under Portuguese domination continue to be deprived of their inalienable right to freedom and independence by the government of Portugal. [Ethiopia had severed diplomatic relations with Portugal July 5, 1963.] The illegal minority regime in Rhodesia continues to subjugate and suppress the vast majority of the African inhabitants of that unhappy land.... The government of South Africa continues to pursue its repugnant and inhuman policy of *apartheid* and has consequently perpetrated the oppression and misery of the African population."

Ethiopia and Liberia had filed a complaint with the International Court of Justice (World Court) Nov. 4, 1960. They charged South Africa with violating its mandate over 318,000-square-mile South-West Africa. The UN General Assembly voted by 86-0 (6 abstentions) Dec. 18 to approve the Ethiopian-Liberian action and by 78-0 (15 abstentions) to call on South Africa to end racial discrimination in South-West Africa. But the World Court in The Hague July 18, 1966 rejected the complaint by 8-7 vote. The court held that neither Ethiopia nor Liberia had "established any legal right or interest in the subject matter of their claim." (By ruling on an "antecedent" issue, the court found it "unnecessary" to decide the plaintiffs' 2 principal contentions—[1] that the League of Nations mandate for South-West Africa was still in force, with the UN assuming the League's supervisory functions, and [2] that South Africa's *apartheid* policy, as allegedly introduced into South-West Africa, constituted a violation of its legal obligations under the League mandate system.) The Ethiopian Foreign Ministry commented that the World Court had "failed to safeguard the rights of freedom and independence of Africans in South-West Africa." It predicted that the verdict would "be inscribed as the most flagrant judgment the court has ever passed on human rights...."

The Republic of the Congo was proclaimed June 30, 1960 after Belgium ended its rule there. Civil war broke out in the newly established country immediately. UN Secy. Gen. Dag Hammarskjold was authorized by the UN Security Council July 14 to send a UN force to the Congo. Ethiopia pledged troops for the UN force July 14, and the first Ethiopian contingent of 460 men left Addis Ababa for the Congo July 17. In a speech before the departing force, Haile Selassie invoked the term "collective security" and compared this action to his sending of troops to Korea in 1950 under UN auspices. By Sept. 1960 Ethiopia had sent 2,572 troops to the Congo. In 1961 4 Ethiopian air force F-84 jets and 700 more Ethiopian troops went to the battle area.

Haile Selassie mediated a border dispute between Morocco and Algeria after clashes between the 2 countries in Oct. 1963. The emperor and the Arab League finally brought the 2 parties together for negotiations Oct. 29, 1963 at Bamako, Mali, with the emperor acting as mediator, and a cease-fire was concluded Oct. 30. The OAU then set up a demilitarized zone between the 2 countries Feb. 20, 1964.

Somali Border Dispute

Haile Selassie's efforts on behalf of African unity are complicated by a troublesome border dispute with Somalia. Somalia claims much of Ogaden Province, an area, with about a million Somalis, on the Ethiopian side of Ethiopia's northern and eastern frontier with Somalia. The Somali government asserts that Britain turned over the disputed land to Ethiopia illegally in 1897 without prior consultation with Somalis. Further problems are created by cross-claims involving Kenya at the section of the border where Ethiopia, Somalia and Kenya meet. Somalia claims Kenya's Northern Frontier District and its 200,000 Somalis. Complications are caused by Somali nomads, who wander across the frontiers without paying tax to any of the disputing countries, and by *shiftas,* armed Somalis accused of attacking Ethiopians. Inconclusive border clashes are frequent occurrences.

Somali government spokesmen said in Mogadishu Jan. 1-2, 1961 that 100 Somali tribesmen and 20 Ethiopian soldiers had been killed in fighting begun in the Damot region of eastern Ethiopia when the Ethiopians fired on tribesmen. Ethiopia charged in a protest Jan. 2 that more than 400 Ethiopians had been wounded in attacks started Dec. 26, 1960 by Somali tribesmen in Ethiopia's Harar Province. Ethiopia charged Jan. 3 that 7,000 Somali tribesmen had carried out an attack on the Ethiopian garrison Dec. 28, 1960. Ethiopian planes Jan. 3 reportedly strafed Somali villages in the Damot area, wounding at least 43 persons.

The Ethiopian Information Ministry disclosed Apr. 9, 1961 that Ethiopian troops had clashed with Somali tribesmen "who crossed over into Ethiopia's Ogaden region from the Somali Republic" to incite residents near the town of Daghabur and persuade them to resist Ethiopian security forces. The ministry said men had been killed by both sides.

At the founding conference of the Organization of African Unity in Addis Ababa May 22-25, 1963, Pres. Adan Abdullah Osman of Somalia raised the question of self-determination for Somalis living in Ethiopia and other countries outside Somalia's boundaries. "Ethiopia has taken possession of a large portion of Somali territory without the consent and against the wishes of the inhabitants," he charged. Ethiopian Prime Min. Aklilou Habte Wold replied: "It is in the interest of all Africans now to respect the frontiers drawn on the maps, whether they are good or bad, by the former colonizers, and that is in the interest of Somalia, too, because if we are going to move in this direction [of suggesting boundary changes], then we, too, the Ethiopians, will have claims to make on the same basis as Somalia, and for more, on historical and geographical reasons."

Somalia was reported Nov. 10, 1963 to have accepted a Soviet offer to supply it with military equipment for an expanded 20,000-man army. Somalia was said to have rejected a small amount of U.S. "defensive" military equipment offered by Washington during negotiations in the summer. Similar military assistance by West Germany and Italy also had been turned down. Dr. Ahmed Mohammed Darman, counselor of the Somali mission to the UN, said in New York Nov. 15 that his country had accepted Soviet arms aid because its "long-standing request for U.S. military assistance was not met." Darman discounted U.S. fears that Moscow's aid would give the Soviet Union a bridgehead into eastern Africa and make Somalia dependent on the USSR. Darman rejected a charge made by Haile Selassie Nov. 15 that the proposed 20,000-man

Somali army "obviously surpassed any reasonable requirement of internal security in a country the size of Somalia," whose population was officially listed at 2 million. Darman contended that Somalia needed a larger army than its current force (estimated at 4,000) because what he described as an additional 8 million Somalis lived outside its borders in neighboring Ethiopia, Kenya and French Somaliland.

Kenya authorities Dec. 6, 1963 reported separate raids on Kenyan territory from Ethiopia and Somalia. Ethiopian raiders were said to have killed 22 tribesmen in one clash near the Northern Frontier District village of North Horr. Kenyan border patrols were attacked 3 times by Somali raiders in the El Wak area in the Northern Frontier District. There had been 13 previous attacks within a month. Kenya declared a state of emergency Dec. 25 along the 440-mile Northern Frontier District border to cope with increasing attacks on military and police posts carried out by tribesmen who allegedly crossed over from Somalia.

A 4-man Ethiopian delegation, headed by Lt. Gen. Merid Mengesha, arrived in Nairobi Dec. 28 to confer with Kenyan officials on the Somali border crisis. (The discussions followed the ratification Dec. 27 of a Kenyan-Ethiopian mutual-defense treaty under which either country would come to the other's aid if attacked by a third party.) A 5-mile "prohibited zone" was established along the Kenyan-Somali frontier by Dec. 29 in an effort to prevent further clashes.

Border clashes involving Ethiopian troops and, at various times, Somali forces or rebellious Somali bands, took place on both sides of the Ethiopian-Somali border during January and February 1964. The Somali insurrectionists had set up a "liberation government" headed by "Prime Min." Mukhtal Taker in Ogaden. An Ethiopian Foreign Ministry report Jan. 16 said that armed Somalis Jan. 11 had killed 15 Ethiopian policemen in a raid in Ethiopian territory. An Ethiopian army patrol then pursued the raiders and killed 43 of them, the announcement said. Ethiopia charged Feb. 7 that Somali military forces had attacked the Ethiopian frontier post of Tog Wajaleh with tanks and heavy weapons. The Ethiopians said that the raiders were routed Feb. 10 after 307 Somalis had been killed and 492 wounded. Ethiopia reported its own losses as "about 10 dead and 44 wounded." In clashes Feb. 11 near Debra

Goriale, 93 Somalis were reported killed. Somalia charged that Ethiopian fighter planes had attacked police posts and towns inside Somalia and that Ethiopian troops had crossed into Somali territory.

The OAU foreign ministers conference in Dar es Salaam Feb. 14 proposed an immediate cease-fire, and the 2 disputants acquiesced Feb. 16. It was announced Apr. 16 that the 2 sides had agreed to withdraw their troops 6 miles from the border.

About 120 persons, were reported Aug. 6, 1964 to have been killed when 200 Merille and Dongiro tribesmen, believed to be Ethiopian cattle rustlers, massacred inhabitants of 10 Turkana tribal encampments in Kenya's Northern Frontier District near the Ethiopian border.

Somalia charged Dec. 9, 1966 that Ethiopian troops had attacked Somali-inhabited villages in southern Ethiopia and that Ethiopian aircraft had bombed and machine-gunned the village of Oddo Dec. 3, 4 and 5. An undisclosed number of people and livestock were reported killed. (Haile Selassie June 10, 1966 had formally opened a US$1.4 million Ethiopian air force jet airfield at Gode, 100 miles north of the Somali border on the Scebeli River.)

The 'Non-Aligned' Nations

Haile Selassie and other African unity leaders participated in many of the deliberations of the "non-aligned" nations— those who refused to take sides in the "cold war" between the Soviet bloc and the West.

Haile Selassie represented his country in Belgrade, Yugoslavia at a meeting Sept. 1-6, 1961 of leaders of 25 "non-aligned" governments. The conferees adopted a 27-point declaration denying that war was inevitable and denouncing colonialism. (The emperor returned to Belgrade Nov. 2-3, 1963 for a state visit to Yugoslavia.)

Representatives of Ethiopia and 46 other "non-aligned" nations met in Cairo Oct. 5-11, 1964 in the presence of observers from 10 other "non-aligned" countries to discuss such world issues as the promotion of disarmament, peaceful coexistence, Western colonialism and the economic development of emerging nations. A communique in the form of a 31-page document, called the Cairo "Program for Peace and International Cooperation," was issued at the conclusion of the conference. One of its major points dealt with U.S.-Cuban relations. The communique "urged" the U.S. to "negotiate the evacuation" of its Guantanamo naval base in Cuba with the Havana government. The U.S. also was called on to lift its economic embargo of Cuba and to negotiate with the regime of Fidel Castro on normalizing relations.

Although Ethiopia had extended full recognition to Israel Oct. 23, 1961, Haile Selassie toured Arab states on a goodwill mission in Oct. 1966. He visited Kuwait Oct. 7-9, and a joint communique announced that Ethiopia and Kuwait had agreed to exchange ambassadors. The emperor visited Lebanon Oct. 9-12. Then, during a visit to Jordan Oct. 12-15, he expressed "sympathy" for the Palestinian Arab refugees. Haile Selassie visited the UAR Oct. 15-18, and he returned to Addis Ababa Oct. 27 after stops in Paris, Geneva and Belgrade.

U.S. Relations

Emperor Haile Selassie visited the U.S. Oct. 1-7, 1963. Arriving in Washington Oct. 1 for a state visit, he was greeted at Union Station by Pres. and Mrs. John F. Kennedy. In a joint communique Oct. 2, the 2 leaders indorsed the drive for African independence and expressed hope "that the final steps to freedom" could be taken peacefully. In a taped "Meet the Press" interview shown over NBC-TV Oct. 6, the emperor called for wider UN participation in African problems and warned that if freedom from "the yoke of imperialism" could not be achieved any other way, African nations might resort to the use of force. Haile Selassie had revealed at a press conference Oct. 3 that he had sent Portuguese Premier Antonio Salazar a friendly message requesting "a definite date" for Portugal's freeing of its territories in Africa. The emperor was given a ticker-tape parade Oct. 4 in New York, where he remained until he left for Canada Oct. 7.

Haile Selassie returned to the U.S. within 2 months because of Kennedy's assassination. While in Washington to attend the funeral, the emperor met Nov. 26 with the new U.S. President, Lyndon B. Johnson.

Sen. Robert F. Kennedy (D., N.Y.), brother of the slain U.S. President met with Haile Selassie in Addis Ababa June 14, 1966. Kennedy's visit was a stop-over on his return from a trip to South Africa.

U.S. aid to Ethiopia continued throughout this period. Figures released by the U.S. in Apr. 1962 revealed that U.S. assistance to Ethiopia during 1952-61 totaled US$99 million; economic aid amounted to $44 million, loans to $47.2 million and agricultural commodity grants to $6.9 million.

The U.S. had lent $23,350,000 to Ethiopia for aviation aid July 17, 1961. With the help of a U.S. grant of $2,220,000, Haile Selassie I University was formally founded in Addis Ababa Dec. 18, 1961. It incorporated several existing institutions, including the University College of Addis Ababa. (By 1966, 3,096 students were enrolled at the university.) The U.S. Agriculture Department announced Aug. 13, 1962 the conclusion of an agreement under which Ethiopia would buy $1.4 million worth of U.S. cotton on long-term credit. The U.S. Agency for International Development (AID) announced in Sept. 1966 a $21.7 million loan to Ethiopia for the construction of a hydroelectric power station on the Fincha River, 100 miles from Addis Ababa. The loan was repayable over 40 years, with a 10-year grace period, at 1% interest during the grace period and 2½% thereafter. A $17,000 AID grant announced at the same time was made available to establish a livestock breeding center in the south, and an additional grant of $170,000 was negotiated to provide water for this project. (U.S. Amb. Edward M. Korry had said in Addis Ababa in July 1965 that American aid to Ethiopia during the next 2 years would total E$100 million.)

The value of Ethiopian exports to the U.S. rose from E$84.4 million in 1963 to E$129.4 million in 1964, the overwhelming export item being coffee. During the same period the value of imports by Ethiopia from the U.S. declined from E$34.4 million to E$26½ million.

277 U.S. Peace Corps volunteers arrived in Ethiopia in Sept. 1962 to serve as teachers. 49 more were placed in the education system in 1963, and 410 more arrived by the end of 1965 and were assigned teaching positions. The volunteers worked on all levels of the education system. According to the Peace Corps training manual of 1968: "Peace Corps Volunteers comprise almost 1/3 of all secondary school teachers and close to half of the core curriculum teachers [in Ethiopia]. . . ."

Other Aid & Foreign Relations

Ethiopia and the Soviet Union announced in Mar. 1960 that the USSR had agreed to build a technical school for 1,000 students as a gift to Ethiopia outside the town of Bahar Dar, Gojam near the source of the Blue Nile. All the construction equipment was supplied by the Soviets. A Soviet-Ethiopian agreement on cultural cooperation, signed in Addis Ababa Jan. 13, 1961, provided for exchanges of scientists, teachers, students, cultural and sports delegations, theatrical companies and tourists.

The International (World) Bank for Reconstruction & Development announced Dec. 31, 1961 that it had lent US$2 million to the Development Bank of Ethiopia to finance various projects. World Bank loans to Ethiopia by the end of 1961 totaled US$25½ million. The World Bank lent US$2.9 million to Ethiopia's Board of Telecommunications June 1, 1962 for the improvement of the phone and telegraph system, and it lent an additional US$4.8 million for the same purpose in Jan. 1966. (The number of phone subscribers in Ethiopia increased from 5,000 to 15,000 during 1955-66.) The World Bank lent Ethiopia US$23½ million July 30, 1964 for the development of electric power.

The International Finance Corp. (IFC), a World Bank affiliate, announced in Nov. 1964 that, in collaboration with Japanese investors, it would help finance the expansion of the Cotton Co. of Ethiopia. The IFC agreed to lend Ethiopia US$1½ million of the more than US$5 million needed; the Japanese export-import bank and 2 Japanese companies agreed to provide the balance. (The value of imports by Ethiopia from Japan rose from E$37½ million in 1963 to E$45.8 million in 1964; Ethiopian exports to Japan in the same period declined from E$8.3 million to E$6 million.)

Italy and Ethiopia Feb. 18, 1963 had concluded an agreement for economic and technical cooperation. It included a US$14 million Italian credit for development projects. The pact was signed during an official visit to Addis Ababa by Italian Foreign Trade Min. Luigi Preti. The Ethiopian parliament rejected another proposed Italian loan June 27, 1964. (The value of Ethiopian exports to Italy declined from E$19.7 million in 1963 to E$18.6 million in 1964, while the value of imports from

Italy in the same period rose from E$44.4 million to E$55.5 million.)

Ethiopia signed the nuclear test ban treaty (Moscow Treaty) Aug. 5, 1963. The treaty banned atomic testing in the atmosphere, in space and under water.

Communist Chinese Premier-Foreign Min. Chou En-lai visited Ethiopia Jan. 30-Feb. 1, 1964 while on a fact-finding trip through Africa. In a communique issued at the conclusion of Chou's visit Haile Selassie pledged Ethiopian support for Communist China's admission to the UN.

Queen Elizabeth II of Britain and her husband, Prince Philip, paid a state visit to Ethiopia Feb. 1-8, 1965. The queen was the first reigning British sovereign to come to Ethiopia. She spent the first 4 days of the visit in Addis Ababa, then toured other parts of the country. (British figures published in Mar. 1965 estimated that Britain's investment in Ethiopia aggregated US$10 million, much of it in gasoline stations and insurance companies. The value of Ethiopian exports to Britain rose from US$9.8 million in 1963 to US$10.6 million in 1964; in the same period the value of imports by Ethiopia from Britain rose from E$25 million to E$26½ million.)

An agreement on technical and financial cooperation was signed by Bulgaria and Ethiopia in Apr. 1965. It provided for Bulgaria to extend a E$12½ million credit at an interest rate of 2½% for the establishment of processing facilities for the meat industry and for the manufacture of building materials and pharmaceutical products. Bulgaria was also helping Ethiopia to develop its fishing industry.

Indian Pres. Sarvepalli Radhakrishnan paid a 4-day state visit to Ethiopia Oct. 10-13, 1965. His busy schedule in Addis Ababa included conferences with Emperor Haile Selassie, diplomatic receptions, talks to military cadets and meetings with the Indian community. Ethiopian officers were serving as members of a 75-man UN India-Pakistan observation mission, which had been sent by the UN to the western border of India and Pakistan Sept. 24 to observe a UN-negotiated cease-fire in the Kashmir dispute.

French Premier Charles de Gaulle conferred with Haile Selassie in Addis Ababa Aug. 27-29, 1966. Their talks were attended by Ethiopian Prime Min. Aklilou Habte Wold and French Foreign Min. Maurice Couve de Murville. In a joint communique issued Aug. 28, the emperor and de Gaulle said that their 2 countries "consider that relations between states should be based on the principles of strict respect for the independence of each and of non-intervention in the internal affairs of others." They "noted that ... there existed between them a broad community of views on international problems. This holds particularly for the problems posed in Africa." They reported that agreements on French-Ethiopian cultural, scientific and technical cooperation had been signed, that the teaching of French in Ethiopia would be expanded and that French experts in urbanization, vocational training, public works and veterinary medicine would be sent to Ethiopia. A technical cooperation agreement had been signed by France and Ethiopia June 5, 1964. It provided for French technicians to assist in town planning and communications projects and to train Ethiopian public works and municipal employes.

Pres. Antonin Novotny of Czechoslovakia visited Ethiopia Nov. 14-18, 1966 and conferred with Haile Selassie. They said in a joint communique that Czechoslovak-Ethiopian cooperation in industry, trade and cultural affairs was "progressing satisfactorily."

Chivu Stoica, chairman of Rumania's State Council, paid a state visit to Addis Ababa Dec. 5-9, 1966. In a communique he and the emperor announced that diplomatic relations between Ethiopia and Rumania would be raised from the ministerial to the ambassadorial level.

The UN Children's Emergency Fund (UNICEF) granted Ethiopia US$1.303 million during 1964-7 for basic health services, community development projects, milk conservation and education.

Policies Clarified

A redefinition of his government's domestic and foreign policy aims was made by Prime Min. Aklilou Habte Wold in a TV and radio address Apr. 13, 1966. He said:

● "In foreign affairs Ethiopia will continue to support with every resource at her disposal the cause of African unity and the attainment of independence by the still subjugated peoples of the world. We shall remain dedicated to the concept of non-alignment, to the principles embodied in the charter of UN and of the Organization for African Unity, to the search for disarmament, to the peaceful settlement of disputes through negotiations, to respect for the territorial integrity of the nations, to non-interference in the internal affairs of others, and the request for universal peace with honor and justice."

● "Ethiopia's potential wealth is vast, but only a small portion of this potential wealth has so far been realized. The land is fertile beyond belief. The possibilities of harnessing the nation's rivers and streams for irrigation and the production of power are enormous." But accomplishing the regime's aims required plans, capital and time.

MODERNIZATION & TRADITIONALIST
OPPOSITION: 1967-71

Struggle Centers Around Tax Reform

A major struggle between forces of modernization and of tradition took place in Ethiopia during 1967. The stage for this battle was Haile Selassie's income tax reform program and specifically his agricultural income tax proposals, which were recognized as a far-reaching attempt by the emperor to restrict the power of the feudal/traditional groups that had for centuries exerted a virtually controlling influence on the politics and economy of Ethiopia.

The draft Proclamation to Amend the Income Tax Proclamation of 1961 was made public by the Finance Ministry in 1966 with the obvious approval of the emperor. Schedule D of this Draft Proclamation No. 255 called for an agricultural income tax system that was fought by the traditional forces from the time the draft was made public. The proclamation, as it finally became law (it was promulgated Nov. 23, 1967), represented an important victory for the emperor in the mere fact of the passage of the agricultural tax. But the major revisions made in the original draft en route to enactment were considered a defeat for Haile Selassie as the embodiment of the struggle for modernization.

Proclamation No. 255 also increased the amount of tax payable on income, on income from rents of lands and buildings and on income from business and professional occupations.

The controversial farm tax proposal, or Schedule D of the 1966 draft, had called for a "tax ... on taxable income which shall be deemed to be the gross income derived from the harvest, diminished by ... the amount of any taxes on lands, the amount of any rent payable, and the deduction of 1/3 of the gross income in lieu ... of production expenses." This tax on income from agricultural activities was to be paid by persons exploiting the lands, "owners or tenants as the case may be."

The Finance Ministry maintained that Schedule D was necessary for numerous reasons. The main argument was that much additional revenue could be obtained, since the various systems of land tenure would be unable to inhibit the enforcement of this tax law. Since no tax on produce had ever been implemented in the past, no exemptions could be claimed based on customary rules of behavior. Although estimates varied radically, employes in the ministry calculated that the increase in revenue would come to a total of between E$10 million and E$100 million annually. The land tax would continue to produce revenue without diminution since the land tax laws remained in effect.

The *Ethiopian Herald* asserted Nov. 23, 1967 that in drafting the tax proclamation, the Finance Ministry, under Yilma Deressa, had hoped to "vastly increase governmental revenue, thus enabling a vast expansion of government services to the people." According to the *Ethiopian Herald,* the agricultural tax proposals were also an attempt "to end the classical system of privileged exemptions." The categories of fertile, semi-fertile and poor land would lose their importance, and land-owners would no longer be able to claim successfully that fertile land was poor land because their produce would show otherwise. The Ethiopian Orthodox Church, although not mentioned in the proclamation, was not specifically excluded, and the Finance Ministry fully expected church lands to be covered by the bill.

Under the proclamation, the differences between measured and unmeasured land became irrelevant, insofar as agricultural income tax was concerned, since the produce rather than the amount of land was the issue. Landowners who had continually prevented land measurement from taking place because of the lower tax on unmeasured land would lose this means of retaining unjustified tax advantages. The draft proclamation, which called for the eventual abolition of the tithe, attempted to ease the burden of the tenant, since the tithe had always been shifted upon him by the landlord. The draft also called for a tax on unutilized land, which would be taxed at the same rate as land adjacent to it. This was largely an attempt to force the cultivation of idle lands.

Schedule D set a tax rate of E$1.50 on taxable farm income up to E$300. The rate rose to E$6 on incomes of E$301-E$480. Rates of E$45 were imposed on E$961-E$1,200 incomes, E$90 on E$1,801-E$2,100 incomes, E$216 on E$3,001-E$3,600 incomes, E$378 on E$4,801-E$5,400 incomes, E$810 on E$8,401-E$9,000 incomes, 10% on $9,001-$9,600 incomes, 15% on E$13,801-E$15,000 incomes and 20% on incomes exceeding E$27,001. A 10% surtax was imposed on taxable income in excess of E$30,000 and an additional 10% surtax on taxable income in excess of E$150,000.

2 assessment procedures were instituted. If books and accounts were kept by the taxpayer, they were used to determine the amount of tax due. In cases where no accounts were kept, the Income Tax Authority in Addis Ababa was empowered to assess the tax by estimation. Power to assess thus remained with the bureaucracy in the capital, but the norms for conducting the assessment were not stated. Once assessment had been made, no reassessment could take place for 5 years, but the proclamation provided for the appointment of a local appeal commission. This appeal commission consisted of the governor of the district (serving as chairman), a district judge nominated by the governor of the province and "3 elders selected by the inhabitants of the place where the land is located." Decisions were by majority vote. The Finance Ministry, in order to obtain revenue during litigation, ordered that, on appeal, "an amount equal to 25% of the tax assessed," or an amount equal to 50% of the tax on the appellant's income of the preceding year, must be deposited with the Income Tax Authority. The proclamation disallowed any further appeal; it specified that "decisions of the local appeal commission shall be final."

Schedule D had been initiated in late 1966 after Finance Min. Yilma Deressa suggested to his advisers at a Finance Ministry meeting that there was a need for a tax on produce. The meeting was attended by Bulcha Demeksa and Tefferi Lemma, the 2 vice ministers. Present also were Ernest Zaremba, the tax adviser, Oscar A. Spencer, the financial adviser, and Eshetu Habtegiorgis representing the legal department. After those at the first meeting had an opportunity to consider the proposal, another meeting was called.

Spencer, the financial adviser, reported that at the 2d meeting "we discussed the option of increasing the land tax, and this was thought best because some thought a new agricultural income tax could not be administered." "I strongly suggested we dive off the deep end and then worry about the problem," he said. "I did, however, suggest that we have a one-year waiting period after the enactment of the bill so that we could avoid problems because of lack of preparation." Zaremba, the tax adviser, was one of those who balked at a new bill. He had estimated that with a new agricultural income tax the number of taxpayers would grow from about 700,000 to 4 million since the new tax would require government collections from tenants. The land tax had previously been collected by the government only from landowners, who collected the tax from their tenants. Zaremba reported: "I had serious doubts whether our administration was prepared to deal with that number of taxpayers. But Yilma said, 'We must start, and we shall overcome these difficulties.'" Some at the meeting argued that a new law was necessary, rather than only an extension of the land tax, since the former was more modern. Under a new law, also, it would be possible "to extend the monetary economy by pushing the monetary sector to individual farmers in outlying areas." This is the major reason that the tax rate was made applicable to those earning E$300 and less per year.

Opinion at the meeting largely favored a new law, and the conservative group represented by Zaremba accepted this consensus. Those present then agreed that the ministry should work out substantive details of the bill and that Eshetu Habtegiorgis should coordinate this operation, putting the various suggestions into a workable bill. During the following months meetings were held, often without Yilma's presence. But he was fully aware of all that was taking place because he and Eshetu worked together.

The measure subsequently produced was, in fact, a land-reform bill since its application did much to make the Church, the landlords and the traditional systems of land tenure conform to some of the norms of 20th century land-use practice. Haile Selassie was kept informed of the framing of the bill but played no role in its actual formulation. On the completion of the draft, it was brought to the emperor for his approval, which he granted. Yilma then ordered the publication of the draft, Proclamation No. 255.

It had been intended that Schedule D of Proclamation No. 255 should go into effect immediately on its approval by parliament. First, however, the bill had to have the approval of the Council of Ministers and the Crown Council. Both of these bodies quickly gave their approval. Thus, by the end of 1966, the bill was ready for presentation to parliament for what the administration hoped would be early ratification.

Prime Min. Aklilou Habte Wold (representing the emperor) and the Finance Ministry presented Draft Proclamation No. 255 to the Chamber of Deputies for consideration in Feb. 1967. Although in the past parliament had occasionally vetoed government bills, what it did with Proclamation No. 255 set a precedent. Parliament, for the first time since its institution in 1955, disassembled and completely reassembled a government bill. In the issue over the agricultural income tax (Schedule D), parliament, and most especially the Chamber of Deputies, established for itself a role in policy-making that it had never taken previously. This action of the Chamber of Deputies was said to have altered the process of official decision-making in Ethiopia. Observers noted that the actions of parliament also clearly illustrated that, as currently constituted, parliament was a major force attempting to stem the tide of modernization.

On submitting Draft Proclamation No. 255 to the Chamber of Deputies in Feb. 1967, the prime minister read the proposals in outline form. Each member had before him a copy of the draft. Yilma and his advisers were present (ministers have the right to attend any meeting of either chamber of parliament). The initial reaction of the chamber was negative (many of the members were landowners).

After the completion of the first reading, the bill was sent to the Economic & Financial Affairs Committee, which reported favorably on the bill in April and sent it back to the chamber with a recommendation for approval. Many members of the chamber, who had had time to study the bill more thoroughly and to discuss it with one another, rebelled against the recommendation and suggested setting up an *ad hoc* committee to study the bill further. A majority agreed, and, after a vote, the *ad hoc* committee was established. The 14 members of the committee were chosen by vote of the chamber. Since it was known which members opposed the bill, the chamber, according to one member, "stacked this committee" by electing individuals who were against the bill. The chamber then voted to send the bill to the *ad hoc* committee for study and recommendation. And during the first months of discussion of Schedule D, the Chamber of Deputies scrapped established procedure in what was described as an attempt to destroy the bill or, at least, to make it as ineffective as possible.

The members of the *ad hoc* committee dealt largely with 4 parts of the draft proclamation: (a) the method of assessment, (b) the tax on unutilized land, (c) the tithe and (d) the rate of taxation. The draft had proposed 2 methods of assessment: (1) if accounts were kept by taxpayers, they would be used to calculate the amount of tax to be paid; (2) but in the majority of cases, where books were not kept, the Income Tax Authority could assess the tax by estimation. The *ad hoc* committee concerned itself mainly with the latter situation.

After a period of discussion and planning with Eshetu Habtegiorgis, the Finance Ministry's lobbyist, this committee's proposal was recommended to the Chamber of Deputies: "There shall be established in each locality an assessment committee composed of 3 members of which 2 shall be elected from among the residents of the locality, as members, and one from among the officials of the district who has adequate knowledge of the locality, as chairman, to assess the tax...." The assessment committee, with 3 members, would be largely controlled by local inhabitants, who would make up the majority on each assessment team. And, of course, the elected members would be the better known members of the community, such as *chiqa shums,* notables and tribal elders. This meant, in effect, that the traditional power groups would control assessment, which would serve the interests of those who supported the traditional order. In what seemed to be an effort to appease the Finance Ministry, the *ad hoc* committee proposed that a E$2 attendance fee "be paid to each member of the committee for each meeting a member will take part in." *Ad hoc* committee members held that the fee system would limit, to some degree, the corruption that the Finance Ministry felt would take place. The 3d member of the assessment committee would, in many cases, be an employe of the Finance Ministry.

The assessment teams were to assess the gross and taxable income of the population in each subdistrict by literally going onto the land. The gross income would be determined by "the harvest on the farm-land from which the income is derived, the types of crops and the produce from such farm-land, [and] local prices of such crops and produce." The basis on which gross income could be determined was amorphous and allowed the assessors freedom of judgment to a very large degree. In fact, as this part of the law was written, assessment teams could base their estimations purely on their own opinion.

The Chamber of Deputies' *ad hoc* committee thus acted to move the power over assessment procedures from Addis Ababa to the interior of the country, where the traditional groups held power, and the Finance Ministry was considered to have lost this first battle over farm taxes.

In addition to altering the assessment procedure, the *ad hoc* committee vetoed the tax on unused land. The committee's publicized objection was that such a tax tended to hurt the small farmer who had less than a *gasha* of land and was probably saving part of his property for his son. But the true reason, it was reported, was that many landlords held many *gashas* of land, much of it unused, and that the new law would force them to pay taxes on it. Eshetu and Vice Min. Tefferi Lemma tried to persuade the committee to uphold this part of the proclamation so that idle lands could be developed and more revenue could be obtained by the Finance Ministry. They also held that forcing the cultivation of idle lands would aid economic development. This tax was vital to the successful application of the agricultural income tax, they said, for otherwise the latter tax could be avoided by keeping land idle, and, in fact, they feared that many large landowners would stop production on some of their land to lessen the burden of the agricultural income tax. Their arguments were rejected, and Eshetu and Tefferi apparently concluded that the *ad hoc* committee was supporting the traditional power blocs in the provinces. This 2d battle thus was also considered to have been won by the Chamber of Deputies.

The original draft proclamation also called for the gradual abolition of the tithe, which was to be kept only until the government could ascertain the amount of additional revenue it was receiving from the agricultural income tax. Although no date was fixed, the tithe was to be abolished when the Finance Ministry decided that the agricultural income tax was being effectively enforced. The Finance Ministry was unwilling to rescind the tithe until it was clear that it was collecting at least the equivalent from the new tax on produce. After listening to Eshetu, who presented the government's viewpoint, the *ad hoc* committee proposed that the tithe be abolished immediately. The committee maintained that the tithe was not a modern tax and that the presentation of the new tax provided an excellent opportunity to end the tithe. An adviser to the land reform and administration minister charged later that the tithe was repealed because the committee felt that "without the tithe, large taxpayers could get away, for a while, without paying either the tithe or the income tax on agricultural production, since it would take a while for the produce from land to be assessed."

The *ad hoc* committee vetoed gradual abolition of the tithe and substituted a new proposal that "upon the date of coming into force of this proclamation, ... the collection of the tithe, with the exception of outstanding taxes, shall be terminated." Before the committee voted on this proposal, Eshetu had attempted to convince the members of the difficulties in enforcing such a provision. It would be almost impossible to prevent landlords from collecting the tithe, he held, and they would keep the revenue themselves. He also argued that communications systems in Ethiopia were so backward that tenants would remain uninformed of the abolition of the tithe and would continue to pay this tax to their landlords. Because the tithe was so deeply rooted in Ethiopian society, it would continue in effect but the government would no longer get the revenue. As Eshetu predicted, the tithe became additional rent that the tenant pays to the landlord, and the understaffed Finance Ministry has been unable to prevent this. Immediate repeal, therefore, was seen as another instance in which the parliamentary committee represented the landlords and as the 3d farm tax battle lost by the Finance Ministry.

The *ad hoc* committee, however, voted to uphold the rate of taxation proposed by the Finance Ministry.

During September and early October 1967 the full Chamber of Deputies debated and voted on each article of the proclamation. By voice votes, it accepted the separate parts of the bill.

The proclamation, as revised by the full chamber, included the original rate of taxation as requested by the Finance Ministry. The ministry's proposal that assessment be controlled from Addis Ababa was rejected and a system of 3-man assessment committees "elected from among the residents of the locality" was substituted. The tax on unutilized land, which the ministry considered vital to the application of the agricultural income tax, was vetoed. The tithe, which the ministry wanted abolished only when revenue from the agricultural income tax was large enough to replace it, was abolished immediately. The appeal commission was accepted as written in the original draft, as was the stipulation that reassessment would take place 5 years after the first assessment had been completed.

The proclamation, as passed by the Chamber of Deputies, provided essentially for an agricultural income tax with a specific rate of taxation on production. The rate was to be decided by an assessment committee controlled from within the interior of Ethiopia, and abuses were to be checked by an appeal commission, also largely controlled from within the interior. The Finance Ministry would be dependent on local traditional forces in its attempt to engage in economic modernization. Conflicts were expected between the traditional and modern forces, and the Finance Ministry was described as deeply displeased with the version of the bill passed by the lower house.

The Chamber of Deputies' version of Proclamation No. 255 went to the Senate in Oct. 1967. Since many senators, like deputies, are landlords, observers noted that they also had an interest in seeing the government proposals defeated. The Senate was, therefore, described as delighted with the new version of the proclamation, and the Senate ratified it by majority vote within the month.

Proclamation No. 255, the new income tax law—including Schedule D, the agricultural income tax provisions—was published in the *Negarit Gazeta* Nov. 23, 1967 and became law.

Farm Tax Problems, Tax Revolt in Gojam

Because of a serious manpower shortage, assessment teams could not be established in each subdistrict. Many teams, therefore, had to assess areas outside of their own subdistricts, and considerable corruption was reported on the part of poorly paid members of assessment committees. Because of this lack of manpower, some overworked teams would skirt some areas and avoid others completely, and in many subdistricts teams would depend on the word of the *chiqa shum* to inform them of the amount of harvest produced per tenant and landlord. The result was a great degree of inaccuracy, and appeal commissions were kept extremely busy. Another problem was weather. If the weather was bad while assessment was under way, the teams would go to another area rather than wait for the rains to end.

In Sidamo Province and other parts of Ethiopia, land remained unutilized until after the assessment was concluded. Thus no tax was charged. Then, for the next 5 years, owners farmed the land free from agricultural income tax. It was reported that tax assessors dared not approach many of the very large landholders because of their political or economic position. The Finance Ministry, with no knowledge of the amount of land owned by these individuals, could do little to rectify the situation.

In Gojam farmers reacted violently when the government sent tax assessors into the province in 1968. There were 2 fundamental reasons for their opposition: (1) Since the government considers payment of land tax one of the means of determining ownership of land, the Gojamies felt that by accepting the law they would be relinquishing their communal land status and would be opening the door to the destruction of communalism. (2) The governor of Gojam, Dejazmatch Tsehai Inqu Selassie, was said to be despised by the Gojamies, who, it was reported, felt that he was unconcerned about Gojam and the people of the province.

When tax assessors initially entered Gojam to estimate the amount of produce grown, many landowners refused to allow them on the land. There was little organization of this opposition, and when fighting did break out in some areas, it was spontaneous. Tax assessors became frightened and frequently sought protection from the territorial army, a small force stationed in each province under the control of the provincial governor. The governor of Gojam, reported to be hostile to the Gojamies, acceded to the request of the tax assessors.

From Dec. 1967 to Apr. 1968 little organized disruption of assessment occurred, and violence was only intermittent. The territorial army seemed to have control of the situation, and although assessors ran into problems in some parts of Gojam, the people of the subprovinces of Agew Midir and Metekel were causing no trouble, and assessment was proceeding as planned.

In May 1968, however, the situation deteriorated. The population of the subprovinces of Bahir Dar, Bichena, Debre Markos, Dega-Damot and Motta, which occupy the eastern part of Gojam, began to organize loosely and to block assessment. A group of farmers who held land in the subprovince of Motta toured the subprovince urging other farmers to prohibit assessment teams from entering their land. Throughout the months of May and June this "organization" spread its doctrine of resistance, but apparently no permanent political structure was established to coordinate this movement. The farmers of Motta, and indeed the people of Gojam, have owned rifles for years. It was not difficult for the activists to convince other farmers that assessment meant the end of communalism and should be stopped. Because the population was armed, it was not difficult for them to persuade assessment teams to stop estimation.

But Gov. Tsehai Inqu Selassie was responsible for seeing that assessment was completed. He informed the tax assessors that they must complete their estimates, and he called upon the territorial army to enter Motta and protect the tax assessors. Bloodshed followed. Many *chiqa shums* who were members of the assessment teams were killed, as were farmers and some members of the territorial army. The number of farmers who had joined the "organization" began to reach into the hundreds, and it was at this point that the "organization" expanded as farmers traveled south to the neighboring subprovince of Bichena in an attempt to persuade the Bichena farmers to join the anti-tax movement.

Gov. Tsehai responded by ordering part of the territorial army into Bichena and insisting that the tax assessors proceed with their job. By early July the farmers of both Motta and Bichena were in a virtual state of revolt, refusing to permit assessment to take place, killing and being killed. Neither the emperor, the Finance Ministry, the Interior Ministry nor the Defense Ministry acted, and the violence continued unchecked.

Following its success in Motta and Bichena, the "organization," which had increased to some 3,000 to 4,000 members, moved west into the subprovince of Dega-Damot, which became the toughest center of resistance. Clashes erupted between the territorial army and organized bands of farmers. Many people were killed and wounded. For all practical purposes, tax assessment and all forms of central government control were at a standstill in the 3 affected subprovinces.

The "organization" then attempted to challenge the emperor directly. Thousands of farmers flocked into Debre Markos, the provincial capital, and asked other farmers to follow the lead of Motta, Bichena, and Dega-Damot. The emperor was informed that if assessment were not halted immediately, the Blue Nile Bridge, which connects Beghemder Province with Gojam, would be blown up. In addition, the leaders of the "organization" demanded the removal of Tsehai from the governorship. It seemed obvious that Motta, Bichena, Dega-Damot, Debre Markos and Bahir Dar (the site of the Blue Nile Bridge) were in revolt.

In mid-July 1968 Haile Selassie and the Defense Ministry ordered some 900 central government troops into Gojam. Most of them went into Motta and Debre Markos, but part of the force was stationed near the Blue Nile Bridge. Their main functions were to stem the farmer movement and to maintain peace. At this time the emperor stopped all tax assessment in the province, but the revolt continued as the "organization" demanded the recall of the governor and the removal of central government troops. Sporadic fighting occurred, and rumors of killing were widespread.

In July Haile Selassie established an executive *ad hoc* committee to review the situation in Gojam and to suggest means of ending the crisis. The committee was made up of Damte Bereded, representing the Finance Ministry, and representatives of the interior minister, the Interior Ministry's

Public Security Department and the Police Department. The committee findings can be inferred from actions Haile Selassie took in August. Assessment in Gojam was permanently halted and assessment teams were disbanded. None of the leaders of the revolt were arrested. The governor was removed, as demanded by the Gojam organization, and many political leaders in the troublesome subprovinces were replaced. The *Ethiopian Herald* announced Aug. 3: "His imperial majesty, Haile Selassie I, today graciously made the following appointments. H. E. Dedjazmatch Tsehai Inqu Selassie, [to be] deputy governor general of Kaffa [Province]; H. E. Dedjazmatch Dereje Makonnen, deputy governor general of Gojam; Fitawrari Ayalew Desta, governor of Motta ...; Fitawrari Ayelew Tadesse, governor of Bichena ..., and Kegnazmatch Makonnen Kassa, governor of Debre markos...."

The emperor May 27, 1969 cancelled all arrears of taxation in Gojam for the previous 19 years.

Cabinet Revised

In the wake of the Gojam tax revolt, Yilma Deressa was removed from the Finance Ministry in Feb. 1969. Haile Selassie announced Feb. 8 that Yilma had been appointed commerce, industry and tourism minister and that Mammo Tadesse had been named finance minister. The Planning & Development Ministry was abolished and its functions transferred to the prime minister's office.

Members of the reconstituted cabinet: Prime Minister—Aklilou Habte Wold. Agriculture—Abebe Retta. Finance—Mammo Tadesse. Health—Ghimatchew Tekle Hawariqt. Foreign Affairs—Ketema Yifru. Commerce, Industry & Tourism—Yilma Deressa. Interior—Zawde Gabre Hiwot. Defense—Gen. Kebede Gebre. Imperial Court—Taffera Worq Kidanewolde. Land Reform—Belete Gebre Tsadik. Communications—Emanuel Abraham. Public Works—Seifu Mahteme Selassie. Mines—Maj. Assefa Lemma. Posts & Telecommunications—Salah Hinit. Information (acting)—Meba Selassie Alemu. Planning (office of the prime minister)—Belai Abbai. Commissioner for Civil Service & Pensions—Tadesse Yacob.

Haile Selassie made the following cabinet appointments Sept. 12, 1969: Justice—Akale-Worq Habte Wold. Education & Fine Arts—Seifu Mahteme Selassie. Chief of Public Security in the Interior Ministry—Col. Belatchew Jemaneh.

The emperor Aug. 19, 1971 virtually retired Yilma Deressa by shifting him from the Commerce, Industry & Tourism Ministry to the post of crown counselor. Ketema Yifru was transferred from the post of foreign minister to Yilma's job as commerce, industry and tourism minister, and Amb.-to-U.S. Minassie Haile was appointed foreign minister.

(Ethiopians in June 1969 had elected 250 Chamber of Deputies members from 2,000 candidates. 70% of the 5,249,000 registered voters cast ballots in this 4th general election. About 68% of the victors were new members.)

5-Year Plan

Ethiopia's 3d 5-year development plan, covering the fiscal years 1968-9 through 1972-3, was published by the Planning & Development Ministry in Jan. 1968. The plan's goal was for the Ethiopian economy to achieve an annual growth rate of 6%, compared with a 4½% rate achieved during the 2d 5-year plan and an average increase of 3% a year in the standard of living. The plan called for expansion at annual rates of 3% in agriculture, 15% in manufacturing and 25% in mining. It scheduled total investments at E$3.1 billion, of which E$2.4 billion was to come from domestic savings and E$715 million from foreign sources.

Government expenditures had reached a level of E$631½ million and government revenues a total of E$611 million in fiscal 1968-9, the year the 3d 5-year plan began. Revenues and expenditures in the preceding fiscal years were (in millions of Ethiopian dollars): 1961-2 revenues—252.8, expenditures—253.1; 1962-3 revenues—283½, expenditures—299½; 1963-4 revenues—359.8, expenditures—359.4; 1964-5 revenues—396.4, expenditures—400.8; 1965-6 revenues—473.3, expenditures—477.7; 1966-7 revenues—496.6, expenditures—453.2.

Ethiopian exports rose to a record level of an estimated E$300 million in 1969 while imports declined to about E$377 million. The resulting unfavorable balance of trade was E$77 million.

Eritrean Rebellion

Rebels of the Eritrean Liberation Front (ELF) intensified their activities against the Ethiopian government beginning in 1967. Killings, plane hijackings and sabotage increased. In one suspected incident of sabotage, more than a million tons of gasoline and oil was destroyed Feb. 27, 1967 in an explosion at the Mobil terminal in Assab (Eritrea).

Anti-rebel activity by the government was also reported at a high level. As an apparent result of anti-insurgency efforts, *Le Monde* reported Sept. 20, 1967, 6 ELF leaders surrendered to Ethiopian authorities in Asmara. Freed under amnesty in accordance with a promise made by Haile Selassie, the rebels told newsmen that they had received guerrilla training in Syria. They and 20 others, traveling on Syrian passports, had entered Eritrea via Jidda, Saudi Arabia and Port Sudan, they said. The rebel admissions added credence to reports of Arab support for the attempt to separate Eritrea from Ethiopia.

The *N.Y. Times* reported Sept. 27, 1968 that Eritrean guerrillas also had apparently lost large numbers of men because of defections and a loss of Arab aid since the Arab-Israeli war of 1967. The ELF was thought by Ethiopian authorities to have fewer than 1,000 guerrillas under arms.

In an action at least partly aimed at the ELF, Haile Selassie Apr. 5, 1969 issued a "Public Welfare & Safety Order" decreeing that trouble-makers could be arrested and held for up to 6 months.

The ELF July 31, 1969 issued a communique warning travelers that they would risk their lives if they used Ethiopian Airlines. The statement warned that the ELF would resort to mid-air attacks in retaliation for Ethiopian air force attacks on Eritrean villages.

A bomb had damaged an Ethiopian Airlines Boeing 707 jet parked at Frankfurt airport Mar. 11, 1969, and several German women who were cleaning the plane were injured. The Ethiopian Foreign Ministry Mar. 13 blamed "certain hate-filled fanatical elements abetted by Syria" for the attack. The Addis Ababa daily *Addis Zemen* said in an editorial Mar. 14 that a "Syrian-Arab organization" had claimed responsibility for setting the bomb. "This band of gangsters," the editorial said, "which works under Syrian direction, has been given the name the Syrian-Arab Movement for the Liberation of Eritrea." Damascus radio reported Mar. 15 that the ELF had claimed to have carried out the Frankfurt bombing because Ethiopian Airlines "transports Ethiopian troops to Eritrea, where they launch savage raids on peaceful Eritrean villages." The ELF asserted that it would continue the attacks.

An Ethiopian Airlines 707 refueling at Karachi (Pakistan) airport was attacked June 18, 1969 by 3 men with submachine guns. The plane's 15 passengers were in a transit lounge at the time of the attack, and no casualties were reported. Part of the plane burned. The police said the attackers, all in their 20s, belonged to the ELF. The terrorists reportedly told police June 19 that they had attacked the plane to dramatize their opposition to Ethiopian rule of Eritrea. The 3 defendants were convicted and sentenced Nov. 21 to a year's hard labor.

6 Haile Selassie University students and an official of the Community Development Ministry hijacked an Ethiopian Airlines DC-3 on an internal Ethiopian flight Aug. 11, 1969 and forced the pilot to land in Khartoum. The Ethiopians requested political asylum in the Sudan. The ELF claimed responsibility for the hijacking.

3 ELF members hijacked an Ethiopian DC-6 with 66 passengers aboard Sept. 13. The plane was forced to land in Aden. One of the hijackers, Mohammed Sayed, 18, was shot by an Ethiopian secret police official who had been a passenger on the flight. The shooting occurred shortly after the plane landed. Police captured the other 2 hijackers. The plane was undamaged and the passengers were unhurt.

2 men attempting to hijack an Ethiopian Airlines 707 were killed Dec. 12, 1969 as the plane flew over southern Europe on the first leg of a flight from Madrid to Addis Ababa. The 2, who were armed with pistols and fused explosive devices, were slain by plainclothes security guards aboard the plane. None of the 15 passengers or 6 crew were harmed. Crew members said Dec. 12 that the men, who were carrying Senegalese and Yemeni passports, had intended to hijack the airliner to Aden in Southern Yemen, but a statement Dec. 13 by the ELF in Damascus asserted that the 2 were ELF members who merely wanted to distribute leaflets to the passengers. Ethiopian sources affirmed Dec. 13 that the men were Ethiopian nationals. Madrid policemen disclosed Dec. 14 that an Ethiopian

student arrested Dec. 10 in the Madrid airport was connected with the hijacking. The student, Ahmed Mohammed Ibrahim, 24, a suspected ELF member, had been carrying a suitcase containing explosives.

The ELF's general command asserted in a statement released in Baghdad Apr. 7, 1970 that the Eritrean Revolution Supreme Council had been dismissed. According to the statement, the council had been away from the battlefield for 7 years and was no longer aware of the fighters' needs. The statement announced that a central general command would supervise and direct the battle from within Eritrea.

A Damascus radio broadcast May 16 said ELF forces had confronted a 3,000-man force of the Ethiopian Imperial Guard along the Red Sea in a 4-day battle during that week. The broadcast said the guard had lost 200 men killed or wounded. The ELF lost 2 men killed and 9 wounded. The report asserted that the imperial forces had "used all kinds of arms and jets."

Eritrean separatists killed Ethiopian Gen. Teshome Erghetu in ambush outside of Asmara Nov. 22, 1970. According to the *London Observer,* the Ethiopian "army struck back, and 15,000 Eritrean women and children fled to the Sudan. Their menfolk were either imprisoned or joined the rebels."

The Ethiopian government declared a state of emergency Dec. 16, 1970 in several areas of Eritrea. It charged that foreign governments had sent armed infiltrators into the area.

The ELF then called for urgent international intervention to end "the mass annihilation of Eritreans" by the Ethiopian army. The London *Times* quoted the ELF Dec. 29, 1970 as claiming that more than 1,000 Eritreans had been killed and many more injured in a massive air and ground offensive by the Ethiopian armed forces since the state of emergency had been declared. ELF Secy. Gen. Osman Muhammed Sabi reported that 37,000 Eritreans had fled to Sudan and that thousands had been left homeless and without food in several Eritrean towns and villages. Dunkalia and Keren, towns in which the guerrillas had their principal bases, had been almost destroyed by air attacks, he declared. The *Times* reported that "a Syrian photographer who spent a month with the rebels recently reported that they moved freely through much of the Eritrean area." The photographer described how in November he had "entered the village of Asciadira, near Keren, with 20 guerrillas who took over the railway station. The guerrillas tore up the rails on a bridge nearby, and the trains, from which passengers had been ordered to disembark, were shunted out of the station and toppled over the bridge into a ravine." According to recent diplomatic reports, insurgents had blown up a bridge on the main road from Asmara to Keren, and 2 bridges were blown up near Agordat on the road north to the Sudan.

Ethiopian High Court Judges Zeroam Kofley and Hadgoug Gilliagabre, who had sentenced ELF supporters to death, had been reported Nov. 27, 1970 to have been assassinated in a bar in Asmara. The assassin escaped.

The London *Sunday Times* reported Dec. 20 that at least 10 Israelis were believed to be working with the Ethiopian security forces in Eritrea against the ELF. (Abel Jacob reported in the *Journal of Modern African Studies* [1971] that "in 1966 the staff of the [Israeli] mission [to Ethiopia] numbered about 100, most of them aiding the [Ethiopian] army but some in the air force or navy." Jacob wrote that the Isrealis helped to train border patrols, and other authorities said the Israelis trained troops fighting the ELF.)

Haile Selassie charged Jan. 18, 1971, that "outside nations and groups" were trying to destroy his empire by supporting guerrillas in Eritrea. He insisted that Eritrea "has always been part and parcel of Ethiopian culture."

The *N.Y. Times* reported Jan. 19 that Libya had "recently" promised to give the rebels US$7.2 million in aid. The *Times* said that the ELF maintained offices in Damascus, Aden, Baghdad, Beirut, Khartoum and Mogadishu.

An Ethiopian Airlines DC-3 with 23 persons aboard was hijacked Jan. 22, 1971 by Eritrean students. It made refueling stops in Khartoum and Cairo before being brought to Benghazi, Libya. The plane was on a domestic flight in Ethiopia when it was seized.

(Police in Addis Ababa had announced Nov. 27, 1969 that they had smashed a bomb plot against the government and had arrested 8 suspects, including an army captain. Police said the plot's leader, Takele Wolde-Hawariat, a hero of the war against Italy, had shot himself.)

Student Unrest

Students in Ethiopia, like those in many other parts of the world, rebelled sporadically during 1968-70 against the traditional order. In some instances the Ethiopian protests violated Proclamation No. 243 of Feb. 11, 1967, which decreed that peaceful public demonstrations were legal only on the issuance by the Interior Ministry of permits stating the time and place of assembly, the route (if any) to be followed and the number of persons involved.

University and high school students rioted and fought with police in Addis Ababa Apr. 1-3, 1968 in protest against the closing of Haile Selassie University's main campus Mar. 30. The school was closed after a violent student demonstration in protest against a campus benefit fashion show in which models wore miniskirts and other Western clothing. Police arrested nearly 100 students during the Apr. 1-3 disturbances. Student demonstrators pelted the police with stones. Prominent Ethiopian women, models and ambassadors' wives were pelted with rotten eggs. Emperor Haile Selassie Apr. 9 ordered more than 2,000 striking students to return to their classes.

Haile Selassie University and all secondary schools in Addis Ababa were closed indefinitely beginning Mar. 3, 1969 on the ground that public order had been threatened by students who were allegedly inciting riots. The students had assailed Education Min. Akale-Worq Habte Wold and had demanded a larger education budget, a change in the scholarship system, the abolition of examination fees, a cut in expenditures for "embassies, banquets and ministerial salaries and travel" and the expulsion of U.S. Peace Corps and Indian teachers.

Students in Addis Ababa began a boycott of schools despite an appeal broadcast Mar. 7 by Haile Selassie, who urged them to return to classes within 3 days. The government Mar. 13 issued a regulation ordering university students taking part in the boycott to return to school by Mar. 17. Failure to return, the regulation said, "will be interpreted as self-dismissal by the students, and the university will not accept them back." The government appealed to parents of secondary school students to ensure that their children returned to classes.

A delegation of the Secondary School Students' Council met with the emperor Mar. 25 to explain the reasons for the boycott. The student leaders said they were striking for: free and equal education for all Ethiopians; fair examinations; the replacement of foreign teachers whose moral standards were "bad" for Ethiopians; reform of the educational system; an increased educational budget that would provide allowances for poor students; and the release of all students who had been detained in the current disorders. Haile Selassie promised that students who could not afford to pay tuition would not have to. He said that the cabinet was studying school reforms but that it would be difficult to provide universal free education and that Ethiopia depended on foreign teachers to staff its schools. He said that the arrested students would be tried through normal legal channels.

Students demonstrated Apr. 3-4 at Haile Selassie University. One student was killed Apr. 3 as he was being transported to a police detention center. The police reported that the student, Demeke Zewde, 20, had been hit by a stone thrown by other students. Police arrested some 500 students Apr. 4 when they held a symbolic funeral for Zewde. Later in the day, more than 1,000 students who had been arrested during the demonstrations were released. Other boycotts and demonstrations were held by high school students Apr. 23-24, and another student was reported killed Apr. 24.

The Ethiopian High Court sentenced 4 students and a teacher Apr. 29 to prison terms of 5 years. They were charged with preparing and distributing pamphlets designed to create unrest and disunity. But the emperor Sept. 8 pardoned all students sentenced to prison or suspended from schools for the disturbances.

(The Ethiopian Foreign Ministry had announced Mar. 13 that 3 Czechoslovak diplomats and 2 Soviet correspondents, from the Novosti Press Agency and Tass, were being expelled for their connection with the student demonstrations.)

3 students were killed and 5 wounded Dec. 29, 1969 when police opened fire against a group of students at Haile Selassie University. The students were resisting police efforts to recover the body of Student Union Pres. Tilahun Gizaw, 29, who had been killed by an unknown gunman. (In Moscow, 60 Ethiopian students Dec. 30 stormed the Ethiopian embassy in protest

against the police action.) The government Dec. 30 ordered the university and all secondary and elementary schools closed. They were not reopened until Jan. 26, 1970.

U.S. Peace Corps Director Joseph Blatchford disclosed in a letter made public Jan. 19, 1970 that 20 of the 338 volunteers in Ethiopia had terminated their service during January "due to reasons of considerable unrest." Blatchford's letter, addressed to Sen. Margaret Chase Smith (R., Me.), said student harassment of Peace Corps teachers had resulted in a cutback in educational programs. Sen. Smith had requested a report after receiving a complaint from a Peace Corps volunteer that he had been beaten by Ethiopian students.

About 30 Ethiopian students occupied the Ethiopian embassy in Stockholm, Sweden Feb. 2, 1970 in protest against what they termed the "fascist regime" of Haile Selassie. The students destroyed books, documents and portraits of the emperor.

Border Problems

Relations between Ethiopia and the Republic of Sudan have often been subjected to strain as a result of incidents in which either (a) Ethiopian forces have pursued Eritrean refugees across the border into the Sudan or (b) Sudanese forces, chasing southern Sudanese opponents of the Muslim North Sudanese regime, have followed their quarry across the border into Ethiopia.

As an example of the sort of charge frequently made, Sudanese Premier Mohammed Mahgoub asserted July 4, 1967 that a force of about 150 Ethiopian soldiers had crossed into Sudan. But Mahgoub denied reports from Khartoum and Cairo that 6,000 Ethiopian troops had invaded the Sudan. Reports from Khartoum July 3 had said that the Ethiopian force had moved into a border area claimed by both countries. The Ethiopian government denied the charge July 3.

Efforts to bring peace to the Ethiopian-Somali border seemed to be at least partially successful during the late 1960s. In a communique published in Addis Ababa and Mogadishu Sept. 22, 1967, Ethiopia and Somalia said they had agreed to "eliminate all forms of tension" between themselves, to establish a joint military commission to examine complaints by either side, and to "perfect cooperation" by means of quarterly meetings of their administrative authorities. The 2 countries Oct. 27 returned aircraft each had lost to the other almost 2 years previously.

Premier Mohammed Ibrahim Egal of Somalia visited Addis Ababa Sept. 1-5, 1968 on Haile Selassie's invitation. The 2 sides agreed to a variety of measures to reduce tensions between the 2 countries and to promote economic and cultural cooperation. In compliance with one of the agreements, Ethiopia called off its 4-year state of emergency along its Somali border Sept. 16.

A series of meetings were held by Ethiopian and Somali delegations July 2, Aug. 13 and Sept. 12, 1969 to discuss ways of improving relations between the 2 countries and of settling future disputes.

After clashes July 8 between Ethiopian troops and Somali civilians at Ramaleh, the Somali Interior Ministry reported July 14 that the conflict had resulted from incidents that had taken place in the area towards the end of June. The 2 governments had begun discussions to prevent similar clashes.

U.S. Relations

U.S. Vice Pres. Hubert H. Humphrey visited Ethiopia Jan. 6, 1968 during a tour of Africa. In an address at Africa Hall, headquarters of the Organization of African Unity, Humphrey said Americans supported the concept of African solidarity.

Emperor Haile Selassie visited the U.S. for 4 days in July 1969 and conferred with Pres. Richard M. Nixon July 7 and 8. During the emperor's visit, demonstrators claiming to be Ethiopians broke into the Ethiopian chancery July 7. State Department spokesman Robert J. McCloskey said July 9 that the U.S. had offered to pay for the $10,000 worth of damage caused by the demonstrators, 14 of whom were arrested. Another demonstration took place across the street from the White House July 8, and 10 persons were arrested for disobeying a police order to disperse.

U.S. State Secy. William P. Rogers visited Ethiopia Feb. 11-12, 1970 during a 16-day tour of Africa. Rogers met with Haile Selassie Feb. 12 and received requests for more U.S. military aid, especially jet fighters.

Testimony by U.S. State and Defense Department officials, made public Oct. 18, 1970, disclosed that the U.S. had entered into an unpublicized agreement with Ethiopia in 1960 to equip and train the 40,000-man Ethiopian army and to oppose any threats to Ethiopia's territorial integrity. In exchange, the U.S. was authorized to expand Kagnew Station, acquired as a global communications facility in 1953. Kagnew, in Eritrea, served as an intelligence station for monitoring communications, particularly within the Soviet Union, and 3,200 U.S. military personnel and dependents were stationed there.

According to the testimony, delivered in June before a Senate Foreign Relations subcommittee on U.S. security agreements and commitments abroad, the U.S. had provided Ethiopia with US$147 million in military assistance since 1953. This represented nearly half the total U.S. military assistance to all African nations in that period. The U.S. also supplied bombs and ammunition used in counterinsurgency operations in Eritrea and in the Ogaden region. Military teams to provide training in counterinsurgency were also sent to Ethiopia by the U.S. This was the sequence of events in the increasing U.S. military commitment in Ethiopia, as reported in the Senate testimony:

● Haile Selassie had approached both the U.S. and the Soviet Union in 1960, asking for increased arms shipments because of a possible threat from newly independent Somalia. The U.S. outbid the USSR and agreed to supply equipment to allow Ethiopia to increase its fighting force from 32,000 to 40,000. Somalia at the time reportedly had a force of 2,000 men.

● In 1962, Somalia applied to the U.S. for arms, but its request was rejected because of Ethiopian objections. Somalia reached agreement with the USSR in 1963 and was given US$35 million in military aid.

● Ethiopia then considered that the threat from Somalia had grown more severe, and in 1964 the U.S. increased its aid. The new aid included a squadron of F-5 fighter planes.

In the 1960 agreement, the U.S. gave certain security assurances to Ethiopia that were finally made public in the testimony released Oct. 18, 1970. Similar assurances had reportedly been given to Haile Selassie, but data on these were deleted from the highly censored testimony on State Department insistence. David D. Newsom, assistant U.S. State Secretary for African affairs and the major government witness at the subcommittee hearing, said the assurances to the emperor contained "no implication of any commitment to defend Ethiopia with American forces." He said the "implication" of the assurances was that the U.S. would use its "good offices in the United Nations in the event of an attack on Ethiopia."

The testimony also revealed that in 1964 the U.S. had sent a 55-man counterinsurgency team to Ethiopia and in 1968 had sent a 12-man team to train Ethiopian forces in civic action. The commander of the U.S. Army's Strike Command—the unit that maintained mobile teams to move into danger spots— visited the emperor at least once a year, according to the report.

Newsom said U.S. military assistance advisory personnel in Ethiopia were under instructions "to avoid involvement in any type of Ethiopian activities against elements within the country." But he acknowledged that arms supplied to Ethiopia as part of the assistance pact were used against insurgents in Eritrea. "What they do with the bombs [provided for training purposes] within their own country is a matter for their decision and their policy," Newsom said.

Sen. Stuart Symington (D., Mo.), chairman of the subcommittee, complained that the extent of the U.S. involvement in Ethiopia had been "as much of a surprise to most citizens as ... to me." Senate Foreign Relations Committee Chairman J. W. Fulbright (D., Ark.) charged that there had been "very artful, in-depth concealment of what we are doing" in Ethiopia. Fulbright said the facts on the 1960 agreement given in "presentation papers" revealed much less than was actually contained in the agreement and the subsequent assurances given to the emperor.

Emperor's Role in Biafran Affair

Haile Selassie was chosen as chairman of a high level advisory mission that was established by the Organization of African Unity Sept. 14, 1967 to express support "for the territorial integrity, unity and peace of Nigeria" during the civil war that followed the Biafran secession.

The emperor and his mission conferred with officials of the Nigerian federal government in Lagos Nov. 23 and agreed on the need to reunify Nigeria. Because the national unity of African states was essential for the greater goal of pan-African unity, the emperor said, "we oppose any attempt at national fragmentation on religious or ethnic grounds." He asserted that "Ethiopia unreservedly supports Nigerian national unity and territorial integrity."

Haile Selassie appealed Dec. 20, 1968 for a one-week truce in observance of the Muslim holiday of Id-el-Fitr and Christmas. The Biafran leaders agreed; but the Nigerian government rejected the proposal and agreed only to short truces (Dec. 21-22 and 24-25) for the 2 holidays.

The emperor, as chairman of the OAU mission, had presided at peace talks between representatives of Nigeria and Biafra in Addis Ababa Aug. 5-Sept. 9, 1968, but the negotiations failed to result in an agreement. There was similar failure in Monrovia, Liberia Apr. 18-20, 1969 when Haile Selassie and his mission oversaw talks between representatives of the warring parties.

The emperor continued his efforts to bring about peace and Nigeria's reunification. These goals were attained, however, only by Biafra's military defeat and surrender Jan. 12, 1970.

Following the Biafran surrender, Haile Selassie was approached by Nigeria and the 4 African countries—Ivory Coast, Gabon, Tanzania and Zambia—that had recognized Biafra. They requested that he use his good offices to bring about a reconciliation between Nigeria and the 4 pro-Biafran nations. After several weeks of discussion and mediation, the emperor announced the reconciliation Sept. 1, 1970.

Other Foreign Relations Developments

Pres. Tito of Yugoslavia paid a visit to Ethiopia Jan. 27-Feb. 4, 1967. He and Haile Selassie "emphasized" in a joint communique "that states, in their mutual relations, should be guided by the principles of peaceful coexistence" and "that these principles, which had been widely accepted in nonaligned countries, contributed towards easing tension and furthering cooperation between states on the basis of mutual respect." The emperor and Tito met again at Tito's summer palace in Brioni Aug. 4-5, 1967. They apparently concentrated on the Middle

East situation, which Haile Selassie described as "of the greatest possible significance" to the Ethiopian government. The emperor paid another goodwill visit to Yugoslavia Sept. 23-26, 1968, and Tito conferred with the emperor in Addis Ababa Feb. 11, 1970. At Tito's initiative, a consultative conference of Ethiopia and 50 other nonaligned nations had been held in Belgrade July 8-12, 1969 to "exchange views on the role of the policy of nonalignment in the present-day world, especially regarding peace, independence and development."

Haile Selassie visited Turkey in Mar. 1967. In a joint communique issued Mar. 6 at the end of his visit, the emperor and Turkey urged immediate independence for all people still under colonial rule.

Pres. Jomo Kenyatta of Kenya paid a state visit to Addis Ababa Nov. 7, 1967 at Haile Selassie's invitation and announced that a road was being planned to link Nairobi with Addis Ababa.

An agreement for Czechoslovakia to help build an Ethiopian tire plant (estimated cost: US$5.8 million) was signed in Addis Ababa in Jan. 1968.

The International Bank for Reconstruction & Development lent Ethiopia US$27 million Jan. 17, 1968 for road construction, US$23.1 million May 9, 1969 for power supply development, US$4½ million June 3, 1969 for communications development, US$3½ million Oct. 22, 1969 for agricultural development and E$7¾ million in July 1970 for the development of the Setit Humera farm project. The Ethiopian government agreed to invest E$3½ million in the latter project.

The *Ethiopian Herald* had reported Nov. 13, 1968 that the UN Development Program had allocated US$1,492,300 for a 5-year adult literacy project in Ethiopia. The project, toward which Ethiopia agreed to contribute $2,956,800, was oriented toward agricultural training for rural development and vocational training for industry.

In 1968 Haile Selassie paid state visits to India Apr. 28-30, to Thailand May 1-3, to Cambodia May 4-7, to Indonesia May 7-13, to Australia May 13-18, to South Korea May 18-21, to Malaysia May 21-24 and to Singapore May 24. In a joint communique issued May 7, the emperor and Prince Norodom Sihanouk of Cambodia announced agreement to establish diplomatic relations and exchange ambassadors. Addressing a joint session of both houses of India's parliament Apr. 30, the emperor had called it futile for advanced nations to spend enormous sums on new weapons while creating defensive systems to counter those very weapons. An agreement for Ethiopian-Indian economic, scientific and technical co-operation was signed by representatives of Ethiopia and India in Addis Ababa June 2, 1969.

Ethiopia, as a member of the UN Security Council, voted Aug. 23, 1968 in favor of a resolution condemning the Soviet-led invasion of Czechoslovakia.

A 5-year agreement for Sweden to help develop Ethiopia's basic school system was signed in Addis Ababa in Aug. 1968. The program called for the construction during 1968-73 of more than 1,000 schools. Sweden agreed to pay at least US$8 million (120 million kroner) of the total US$14 million estimated cost of the project.

Queen Juliana and Prince Bernhard of the Netherlands paid a state visit to Ethiopia in Jan. 1969. They were entertained by Haile Selassie, became honorary citizens of Addis Ababa and inspected a Dutch-run sugar estate and factory at Wonji.

Haile Selassie paid a 2-day state visit to Guinea Apr. 20-21, 1969 and a similar visit to the UAR June 14-15, 1969. The emperor and UAR Pres. Gamal Abdel Nasser conferred on the Middle East situation, on relations between the 2 countries, on the consolidation of the Organization of African Unity and on its role in promoting African cooperation.

Israeli Foreign Min. Abba Eban met with Haile Selassie in Addis Ababa June 28, 1969 while on an official tour of East Africa. An agreement for the cultivation of cotton in Ethiopia by a specially formed joint company was signed in Aug. 1969 by the Ethiopian National Development Co. and Elda of Israel. The cotton was to be grown on a 5,000-acre farm 125 miles south of Addis Ababa, and a 5-man Israeli team was to manage the project. Most of the equipment, fertilizers and pesticides were to be bought in Israel.

Ethiopia signed the nuclear nonproliferation treaty Mar. 5, 1970.

West German government loans for the construction of a road from Dilla to Moyale were increased in mid-1970 from 37.4 million Deutschmark to a new total of 46.9 million.

Haile Selassie paid an official visit to Rome Nov. 6, 1970. This was his first visit to Italy since the Italian-Ethiopian war; it was intended to signify the final rapprochement between the 2 countries.

Communist China's first ambassador to Ethiopia, Yu Pei-wen, presented his credentials to the emperor in Addis Ababa May 19, 1971. Dr. Makonnen Kebret was named by the emperor to serve as Ethiopia's first ambassador to Communist China, and he took up his post in Peking Sept. 11.

Haile Selassie visited Communist China Oct. 6-13, 1971. He conferred Oct. 8 with Chinese Communist Party Chairman Mao Tse-tung and met repeatedly with Premier Chou En-lai. While the emperor was in Peking, Communist China agreed to lend $84 million to Ethiopia for economic development and 2 Ethiopian-Chinese treaties—on economic and technical cooperation and on trade—were signed Oct. 9. At a welcoming banquet in Peking Oct. 6, Haile Selassie had lauded Mao, whose "life history," he said, "is in essence the life history of the new China." Mao's "outstanding achievements in organizing and leading ¼ of the human race have earned him an unassailable peace ... in world history," the emperor declared. "The depth and scope of Chairman Mao's thoughts have achieved for him a place of honor among the great thinkers. His examples shall live to inspire many generations to come." "Ethiopia has recognized that the government of the People's Republic of China is the only legal government representing the entire Chinese people and has consistently supported the restoration of all its legitimate rights in the United Nations," Haile Selassie continued. "The idea of excluding China from membership in the United Nations has been firmly opposed by Ethiopia." He said he had come to China to discuss ways of achieving "much wider [Ethiopian-Chinese] cooperation in the interest of our 2 people."

INDEX